MW00436488

Life of General John Sevier

Francis Marion Turner

JOHNSON CITY, TENNESSEE

ISBN 1-57072-058-4
Copyright © 1910 by The Neale Publishing Company
Reprinted 1997 by The Overmountain Press
Printed in the United States of America

1 2 3 4 5 6 7 8 9 0

CONTENTS

PUBLISHER'S ACKNOWLEDGMENT

Photographs and illustrations on pages xi, xii, and xiii were made available for this reprint through the courtesy of Ella Pierce Buchanan, Lynn Fox, Cherel Henderson, Mildred Kozsuch, Nancy Sevier Madden, Tom Windle, and Peter Zars. Numerous helpful suggestions were an encouragement to publish this reprint; and in the process, a few obvious errors in the original text were marked for correction. It should be noted that the monument inscription quoted on page 128 has John Sevier's birth year as 1744. His son, Col. George Washington Sevier, wrote Lyman C. Draper, historian and author of *King's Mountain and Its Heroes*, that the year was 1745. Since 1744 is on the monument and the inscription is properly quoted "as is," no change was made in that date.

PREFACE TO BICENTENNIAL REPRINT

During the bicentennial year, it is important that we honor our first governor and recognize that John Sevier was the moving force in the establishment of the state of Tennessee. From protecting the early settlers from Indian attacks to entertaining government officials and his neighbors on the Nolichucky, Sevier was certainly the most outstanding man in early Tennessee history. The reprinting of this book is one way we can honor his memory and recall his accomplishments.

John Sevier first visited what is now Northeast Tennessee in 1771 when he stopped at Sapling Grove (Bristol) and traded with Evan Shelby who kept a store at that place. In 1772 he returned and attended a horse race at Watauga Old Fields (Elizabethton). Sevier traveled back to his home in Virginia, sold his land, and in early December of 1773, he and his family left Millertown and traveled down the Shenandoah Valley to the Holston River Settlement, arriving on Christmas Day. He built a home at a site at the end of River Bend Road, off Hickory Tree Road in present-day Sullivan County. This lovely site is now six miles from Bristol and ten to fifteen miles east of Blountville. The birth record indicates that a son, Richard, was born there.

Sevier became interested in the Watauga Settlement, accepted a position as one of the commissioners, and was probably a clerk of the Watauga Association. He assisted in building Fort Watauga (Caswell) and was a lieutentant when the fort was attacked in July 1776. His wife Sarah remained at home on the Holston River and fled with the children to John Shelby's fort for protection. It is thought that later in 1776 John Sevier moved his family to the Watauga Settlement where a daughter, Rebecca, was born in 1777.

Samuel Cole Williams's book *Dawn of Tennessee Valley and Tennessee History* has a list of the early settlers' home sites taken from extant records of entries and deeds executed in 1775. These records show that Sevier had land in the following locations:

(1) South side of Watauga near the mouth of Stony Creek, adjoining Teter Nave, running to Lynn Mountain, 640 acres.

(2) John Sevier and John Carter "in conjunction" on Stony Creek on both sides, 490 acres.

(3) John Sevier on the Holston River adjoining Edward Cox, 640 acres.

(4) John Sevier and John Carter adjoining their former tract, 280 acres.

His homesite was probably entry (1), close to the Carters' residence. The two families were close friends during the early settlement of the state. The Carter home, built about 1780, has been restored by the state of Tennessee and is open for tours.

About 1777-78, John Sevier moved his family again—this time to Limestone Creek (Telford) in Washington County. He had a mill on Limestone Creek, and two of the millstones can be seen today in the yard of the home opposite the mill site. Three of the children, Nancy, Catherine, and George Washington, were born there.

It was in 1780 while living on Limestone Creek that Sarah, his first wife, died on a cold February day. Her exact place of burial is not known; however, the writings of John Fain Anderson, in his scrapbooks, relate this story: John Stuart, a surveyor, told him that Mrs. Sevier was buried in the old Wattenbarger Cemetery along the railroad track, just west of Telford. When the railroad tracks were laid in the early 1850s, some of the remains were moved to the Payne Town Cemetery (Ernest Chapel Methodist Church Cemetery) nearby. Other bodies remained buried near the tracks at the Wattenbarger Cemetery. Sarah was not buried at the Salem Presbyterian Church Cemetery as it did not exist in 1780 when she died.

In 1783 Sevier moved his second wife, Bonny Kate, and his children to the Mount Pleasant plantation, south of the Nolichucky River. A land grant for 640 acres to John Sevier, dated November 10, 1784, included the plantation where John Woods formerly lived and several islands in the

Nolichucky River. Joanna, Samuel, and Polly were born during the period of the State of Franklin, 1784-1788. Letters Sevier wrote during this period show Mount Pleasant as the place of residence.

To secure a debt and interest then due, Sevier mortgaged Mount Pleasant to Alexander Baine of Botetourt County, Virginia, January 10, 1788. The 640 acres were deeded to Baine for 1,000 pounds Virginia money in August 1788 and were described as the "same estate where the said John Sevier lived." Later in 1805-1808, Samuel Jackson, a merchant from Philadelphia and former resident of Nashville, purchased the Mount Pleasant plantation after a court case.

After selling Mount Pleasant to Alexander Baine, John Sevier and his family moved north across the Nolichucky River to Plum Grove which was purchased from John Clark, Sr., of Georgia on October 7, 1790. The land was described as 226 acres between John Weir and John Redding. In a separate deed at the same time of the above deed, Sevier acquired 37½ acres, and on March 4, 1793, he purchased John Redding's 250 acres when Redding moved to Georgia.

Plum Grove remained the home of John Sevier and his family during his first three terms as governor, 1796-1801. During the week while he carried out his duties in Knoxville, he rented various quarters; however, he frequently came home on weekends to be with his family at Plum Grove, according to statements in his diary. Two children, Eliza Conway and Robert, were born at Plum Grove.

In April 1803 John Sevier moved his family to his Marble Springs home below Knoxville after his Plum Grove plantation was sold to John Nelson. A year later William Tyler obtained the plantation for $1,500 through a case in the U. S. District Court. Plum Grove was owned by the Tyler family for many years. In 1903 John Graham purchased Plum Grove which is now owned by his daughter, Sarah Lou Dillow. About 1908, Judge Guy S. Chase bought the Plum Grove house, had it torn down, and used several of the oak logs for making canes.

Valentine, son of John Sevier, lived near or at the Marble

Springs plantation before Gov. Sevier moved to the home in 1803. Several entries in his diary indicate he was constructing farm buildings and farming the land during his last terms as governor.

The death of John Sevier occurred near Fort Decatur, Alabama, on September 24, 1815, while on a mission for President James Madison. It was not until 1889, during the first term of Gov. Robert L. Taylor, that Sevier's remains were returned from Alabama to Tennessee and buried on the lawn of the Knox County Courthouse. A large monument marks his grave, and nearby are markers for Sarah Hawkins and Bonny Kate.

After Sevier's death in 1815, Mount Pleasant remained in the possession of Samuel Jackson until 1826 when he deeded the plantation to his son, Alfred E., who later became a Confederate general. In his will, in 1880, Gen. Jackson bequeathed the plantation to his son, Henry Jackson, who lived there until his death in 1914.

The will of Henry Jackson states, "I give and devise to my three nephews, James T. Carter, William D. Fuller, and Fred J. Fuller my Chuckey River farm on which I now reside, containing 640 acres and to their heirs and assigns forever." It is not known when the heirs of Henry Jackson had the original John Sevier log house torn down.

The late Col. James Corbitt, descendant of the Seviers, had a photograph of Mount Pleasant, taken by Nashville photographer Marvin Wiles. The picture was made either at the homeplace on the Nolichucky or in Nashville at the Harpeth Hills Hunt Club where the house had been moved. Mount Pleasant is reported to have burned in the late 1920s at the hunt club.

For a number of years there has existed an error in the locations of the Mount Pleasant and Plum Grove plantations. Carl Driver wrote a biography of John Sevier in 1932 and mentions Sevier's move to the Nolichucky. He states, "On the bank of the Nolachucky River he built his homestead— he called it a plantation—and named it Plum Grove." This statement evidently confused people and caused them to think that Plum Grove was near the bank on the south side of the Nolichucky when in fact it was Mount Pleasant. The John Sevier Chapter of the D.A.R. was evidently influenced by Driver's statement when in 1934 they dedicated a monument located on State Hwy. 107 across from the entrance to Jackson Bridge Road. Recognizing John Sevier's home on the south side of the river, the monument reads:

Plum Grove
Home of
Gov. John Sevier
Stood on hill 125 yds. N.W.
Erected by John Sevier Chapter D.A.R. 1934
Limestone from original chimney

Recently a title search and entries in Sevier's diary have proved that "Plum Grove" on the monument should be "Mount Pleasant." The Plum Grove site is located on the north side of the river about a mile away across Jackson Bridge on the Dillow property. Members of the John Sevier Chapter have agreed to allow the name on the monument to be changed to Mount Pleasant. The Washington County Historical Association has purchased a metal casting with the inscription, "Mount Pleasant," to cover "Plum Grove." It is hoped that this change can occur soon to clear up the confusion on the locations of the two homes of John Sevier on the Nolichucky.

Mrs. Elizabeth Fuller Sanders, daughter of Fred Fuller, inherited part of the farm and purchased other tracts from relatives in June 1949 in order to keep the tracts intact as the original Sevier grant. In 1967 she sold the Jackson farm (Mount Pleasant) to Thad and Jack Wiseman and their wives. The U.S. Forest Service of the Dept. of Agriculture purchased the farm July 16, 1970, as one of the last original land grants in Washington County.

When the Forest Service bought the Mount Pleasant site, it included a large frame house and several outbuildings. These buildings were either torn down or burned, and the property has grown up in tall weeds. Even the remaining chimney of Mount Pleasant cannot be seen because of the weeds and vines.

An attempt has been made to include the Mount Pleasant site on the National Register of Historic Places during the bicentennial year. At the time of the reprinting of this book, no word has been received from the U.S. Forest Service or the Tennessee Historical Commission that the site has been nominated for the National Register.

References

Driver, Carl S., *John Sevier, Pioneer of the Old Southwest.* Chapel Hill, North Carolina, The University of North Carolina Press, 1932.

Johnson City Press-Chronicle, Aug. 12, 1970. Smith, Paul R. "Government Buys 671 Acres Along Nolichucky." p. 1 & 16.

Sevier, Cora and Madden, Nancy Sevier, *Sevier Family History with the Collected Letters of General John Sevier, First Governor of Tennessee.* Washington, D.C., 1961.

Washington County Tennessee Court Records. Will Books 2 & 4. Various deeds.

Watauga Association of Genealogists. *History of Washington County, Tennessee.* Madden, Nancy Sevier, "John Sevier's Home on the Nolichucky." p. 483 & 484. The Compiler, 1988.

Williams, Samuel Cole, *Dawn of Tennessee Valley and Tennessee History.* Johnson City, Tennessee, The Watauga Press, 1937.

MILDRED KOZSUCH, CO-CHAIRPERSON
WASHINGTON COUNTY BICENTENNIAL COMMISSION
JONESBOROUGH, TENNESSEE
1996

Portrait of Bonny Kate Sevier, second wife of John Sevier, was painted by Lloyd Branson of Knoxville from descriptions given him by her many descendants.

Monument for Bonny Kate Sevier, second wife of John Sevier, stands on the Knox County Courthouse lawn in Knoxville. Her remains were moved from Russellville, Alabama, and reinterred here July 27, 1922.

King's Mountain monument near Gap Creek in Carter County.

Plaque on the front side of King's Mountain monument.

Monument for Sarah Hawkins, first wife of John Sevier, was erected in 1946 on the Knox County Courthouse lawn in Knoxville by Sarah Hawkins Chapter, D.A.R., Tennessee Historical Commission, and Sevier descendants.

View from the back of Marble Springs, John Sevier's home during the last years of his life. It is located east of Knoxville on Neuberts Springs Road.

On June 15, 1889, this monument was placed on the Knox County Courthouse lawn in Knoxville to mark the grave of John Sevier.

This photograph of John Sevier's Mount Pleasant home was made about 1910 by Marvin Wiles, a Nashville photographer. It is uncertain whether it was made at its orginal location on the Nolichucky River in Washington County or after it was moved to the Harpeth Hills Hunt Club in Nashville.

Portion of a cane, now owned by Jeremy Dykes, made from a log of John Sevier's Plum Grove home.

The last home of John Sevier in Washington County, Plum Grove was located on the north side of the Nolichucky River a short distance from Jackson Bridge and the Conklin Community. It was used as a tobacco barn before it was torn down about 1908. Guy Chase, who bought the huge oak logs, had canes made from some of them. The farm is now owned by Sarah Lou Dillow.

One of the original cabins at John Sevier's Mount Pleasant plantation on the south side of the Nolichucky River, this structure was torn down in the 1970s. The property was also known as the Jackson Farm before it was sold to the U.S. Forest Service in 1970.

Visiting the John Sevier grave site in Decatur, Alabama, Tennessee's Governor Robert Love Taylor, with his arm on one of the bars, is standing on the left. Governor Thomas Seay of Alabama is on the right.

When the remains of John Sevier were moved from Alabama and reinterred on the County Courthouse lawn in Knoxville, Tennessee, on June 15, 1889, 30,000 attended the service and heard Governor Robert Love Taylor give the address.

Preface

When a boy reads the biography of a great man, he is especially interested in the hero's boyhood days—his joys and sorrows, struggles and victories; and he is always disappointed if nothing has been said about that period of the hero's life. The fact that the youthful period of Sevier's life had been neglected, led me to write this little volume. During my school days, when I read about the wonderful battles which General Sevier fought with the dusky warriors of the forest, and about the terrible clash with the British at King's Mountain, I wondered if anything reliable had been written about his boyhood days. Later I was disappointed to find that the biography of an American hero, a man who had been instrumental in turning the tide of the Revolution at King's Mountain, had been sadly neglected. In all my early investigations I could not find a book that furnished the information I was seeking. I read Ramsey's "Annals of Tennessee" and Gilmore's "Rearguard of the Revolution" and "John Sevier as a Commonwealth-Builder," the last-named not being a biography and very unreliable history; these books, though full of interesting matter, did not give me enough about the early life of General Sevier and about other neglected parts of his interesting career.

Next I wrote letters of inquiry. By this plan I found, in the Draper Manuscript Collection in the State Historical Society of Wisconsin, many letters and manuscript statements containing much desirable information about Sevier. In 1844, Doctor Draper visited three sons of General Sevier and had personal interviews with them, taking notes of the information he gathered. He also received many letters from them, some of which contain much biographical and genealogical material. It was pure love for historical investigation that led the venerable Doctor Draper thus to preserve for mankind much information of this kind. This is the first time this valuable manuscript matter about Sevier's life has been presented in history or biography.

This book was written for those who love to read about

the deeds of the heroes who fought for our freedom and caused the light of peace and civilization to shine upon our "land of the free and home of the brave." My thanks are due to Mr. L. C. Burke, Librarian of the State University of Wisconsin, who went through the Draper manuscripts carefully and copied for me such material as I desired. My thanks are also due to Doctor Reuben Gold Thwaites, the well-known author, who, as Secretary of the State Historical Society of Wisconsin, very kindly aided me with information concerning the Draper manuscripts. I must also thank Doctor E. W. Kennedy, Professor of History in the Peabody College for Teachers, Mr. A. V. Goodpasture, author and Secretary of the Tennessee Historical Society, Mr. J. W. Shepherd, Nashville, Author, and Doctor Arthur Howard Noll, of the University of the South, Sewanee, who kindly read my manuscript and made suggestions and corrections.

FRANCIS M. TURNER.
CHRISTIANA HIGH SCHOOL, April 24, 1909.

CHAPTER ONE

The Sevier Family

In the sixteenth century the town of Xavier, in Navarre, in the French Pyrenees, gave its name to the family of one of its most famous citizens, upon whom the Roman Church a century later conferred the title of Saint. St. Francis was of noble parentage and was born in the castle of Xavier on April 7th, 1506. He was educated at the College of St. Barbe, Paris, and during his student days he became acquainted with Ignatius de Loyola. Some years later these two, with others, founded the Society of Jesus, or the Order of the Jesuits, as it is usually called. St. Francis was afterwards sent by the Order to the East as a missionary. He visited Japan and many of the islands, and, with his staff of assistants, baptized in a single month ten thousand natives of the little kingdom of Travancore. He died in 1552 on his way to undertake a mission to China. Seventy years later he was canonized, that is, declared by the Roman Church entitled to be called Saint Francis, though he is generally known as the "Apostle of the Indies."

About this time the Protestants of France, called Huguenots, were becoming numerous and powerful, despite the persecutions to which they were subjected in the reign of Francis I and the famous massacre of St. Bartholomew's Day, August 24th, 1572. They were the Puritans of France and were generally noted for their virtuous conduct and the purity of their lives. In 1598 King Henry IV of France issued the Edict of Nantes, which secured to them full political and civil rights and protected them from persecution. In 1685 Louis XIV revoked the Edict, and the persecution of the Huguenots began again and was pursued with such violence as to force hundreds of them into exile in Prussia, the Netherlands, Switzerland, England, and America, or wherever the rights of Protestants were respected.

Strange as it may seem, some of the family of St. Francis Xavier, living at Xavier, and bearing the name of the town as a family name, had embraced the Protestant religion, and one of them, a devout young Huguenot, was among the first to leave France after the revocation of the Edict of Nantes. He settled in London and there the family name of Xavier was gradually changed to Sevier. He married a woman named Smith, by whom he had a son, born some time in the year 1703. In or before 1740, this son, Valentine Sevier, ran away from home and came to the New World. He found a home in the beautiful Shenandoah Valley, Virginia, in what was then Augusta County, but is now within the limits of Rockingham County.[1]

In course of time Valentine Sevier met Miss Joanna Goade,[2] and some time later married her. It was a very happy marriage and the two were held in high esteem by all the neighbors and friends. On September 23, 1745, this marriage was blessed with a son, to whom the name John was given. Little did these young parents fancy their babe would live to be one of the world's heroes; little did they think then that he would one day help to smite the enemy of his country and make way for peace and civilization; little did they dream, perhaps, that he would ever be a ruler among his people, General John Sevier.

Valentine Sevier, John's father, had a country store, a small mercantile business, and a farm; and his son John was taught to labor in the field, learning the noblest of occupations. John was very fond of horses and dogs, and living on the frontier of the colony, near the region of wild game, he also became exceedingly fond of hunting. When tired of the monotony of farm life, nothing pleased him more than to shoot squirrels and turkeys

[1] Draper MSS.
[2] Draper MSS.

in the mountains or, in company with his boy friends, to mount his favorite horse and ride away into the distant woodlands with the pack of hounds for a fox-chase or a deer-hunt. The yelping of the hounds was fascinating to him, and he would put the spurs to his horse and gallop away to some high hill to listen to the music of the chase. Hunting wild game developed his powers as a marksman, and riding the chase gave him the fine physical form for which he was distinguished in after life as a soldier and general.

In Sevier's youth the South had no public free schools, though there existed in most communities the "old-field school," supported by those who chanced to have an interest in it. But at best this was a very poor place to obtain an "education." The school-house, built of logs and daubed with mud or mortar, was often so open in construction that school could not be kept in it during the winter months. It was furnished with benches made of slabs hewed from split logs, each slab resting upon four legs driven in auger holes, two at each end. An opening or two, made in the wall of the building and furnished usually with wooden shutters, served as windows, and a "stick and dirt" chimney formed a very wide fire-place at one end of the room.

As for the teacher, he was usually a stern old fellow whom the scholars feared rather than loved or respected. He was much more skillful in the use of the rod than in imparting knowledge, for he had very little learning to impart. Spelling and writing, a little grammar, and a smattering of arithmetic were about all he could teach. He usually had a long list of rules which he read daily to his pupils for the regulation of their conduct, and often some unfortunate pupil who had violated the "rules" had to wear the "dunce cap" or was caned. There were no copy books, except what the schoolmaster and his pupils contrived to make of fool's cap paper. Pens were made of goose-quills. The schoolmaster was very skillful in making these pens and in "setting copies" for his pupils and then the stern voice of the old master, followed by a rap on a bench, awakened some idle pupil to greater efforts to get his lesson. But there existed throughout the country a few academies and private schools in which some of our greatest patriots and statesmen were educated after they had left the oldfield schools. Books were rare in the colonies, but well read. Shakespeare, a few volumes of history and biography, and the Bible comprised the library of the frontier settlements.

In spite of these drawbacks young Sevier was fairly well educated for his time. He was a student for some time in the academy at Staunton, Virginia, and applied himself with reasonable diligence and acquired a good knowledge of English, as his subsequent correspondence shows. While attending school at Staunton, he fell into a mill race one day and would have been drowned had he not been rescued by two ladies, sisters, one of whom was later the wife of Governor Matthews of Georgia.[3] As long as he lived, whenever opportunity offered, he showed his gratitude to these ladies for their rescue of him in his youth.

When his school days were over, John returned to his home and became a clerk in his father's store.[4] His father had become somewhat dissipated and spent a good part of his time at Culpeper Court House, gambling and drinking. Such indulgences were very common in those days and were not regarded in the way they are at present. Fortunately John never had any such bad habits, and was not even addicted to the use of tobacco. He had pleasant manners which won him many friends, and he was naturally kind and courteous to his customers; best of all, he was so honest and sincere that he had the respect of all with whom he was associated.

About the time young Sevier was attending school at Staunton, Benjamin Franklin was postmaster-general, the mail was beginning to be carried by stage-coaches, cities were growing rapidly, and there were seven newspapers published in the colonies. Many planters read the papers and kept informed on the political, social, and religious topics of the day. Books by American authors were beginning to be read. Franklin's wise sayings in "Poor Richard's Almanac" were eagerly read by people in all the colonies. It was not by any

[3] Draper MSS.
[4] Draper MSS.

means a time of mental stagnation; the tide of political, social, and religious affairs forced the minds of men to great activity. The school days of Sevier ended at Staunton. William and Mary College was the best-equipped of the colonial institutions of learning, and it was customary for the sons of the better class of planters who desired an education to enter that institution for their degrees and training for professional life. But study was irksome to John Sevier's active nature, and he did not enter William and Mary. He seems not to have aspired to distinction in a professional career in the fields of science or literature. His was the mission of the soldier and statesman, and he was to become one of the pioneers of civilization in its westward journey.

A great many wild tales are told of Sevier's fights with the Indians in his youth; and, while we cannot rely upon them all as true, we do know that he grappled with the dusky fellows while yet in his teens. In a letter to Doctor Draper in 1844, Major James Sevier, son of John Sevier, says of his father: "Near the close of the old French war, Sevier was out on several scouts on the Virginian frontiers and on one occasion, with others, came near getting into an ambuscade, but fortunately discovered the net in good time to escape. This was his first military service and experience."[5]

After leaving the academy at Staunton, and while yet a merchant in his father's store, young Sevier began to devise plans for launching out into the sea of life in his own little bark. Like many another American, he had learned early to paddle his own canoe. The cause of such serious considerations, suffice it to say, was the fact that he had fallen in love. This passion of love, growing stronger day by day, may have been one of the chief causes of his leaving the academy and ending his school days when he did. History is silent as to this. He seems to have been devoted entirely to the young woman, Sarah Hawkins. She was a tender, delicate young lady; and her delicacy and pure modesty constituted the youth's ideal. She may have been a schoolmate, and was doubtless the first lover of his youth. The wedding took place in 1761.[6]

[5] Draper MSS.   [6] Ibid.

After this union, which proved a happy one, young Sevier tried his hand at farming on a tract of land called Long Meadows.[7] This work was well suited to his taste, as he could here indulge his fondness for horses and dogs and hunting more freely than he could if engaged in the mercantile pursuits. Those who have enjoyed the freedom and independence of farm life, and the peace and happiness which dwell in the humble cottage, can easily imagine the supreme happiness of this young husband and wife on the little farm at Long Meadows.

Sevier's business at Long Meadows was on too small a scale to satisfy his ambitions and he remained there only a few years. He bought a tract of land in the Shenandoah Valley, near Mt. Jackson, and laid off town lots, founding a little town which he named New Market, and which still exists under that name, and has a population of about seven hundred. In this town he established himself as a farmer, inn-keeper, and merchant. He gave the Baptist Church three acres of land on which to erect a church building. He dealt in dry-goods, groceries and such other articles as were in demand, the settlers along the valley and from the hills proving good customers. It often happened that the Indians came down from the mountains and exchanged their peltries for beads, looking-glasses, gay-colored cloths, and such other things as were attractive to them.

Sevier remained in New Market several years and prospered, but, desirous of doing greater things in the world for his wife, and rapidly increasing family, he began to yearn for a new field of activity. So, in 1770, he moved to Millerstown in Shenandoah County,[8] only a few miles from New Market. While living here he began to travel and explore. Formerly he had been seeking his fortune in the northern part of the Shenandoah Valley; now he turned his attention towards the wilderness of the great Southwest in the region known to-day as East Tennessee.

[7] Ibid.   [8] Draper MSS.

CHAPTER TWO

Early Settlements in East Tennessee

Before considering the early settlements in the regions now known as East Tennessee and the advent of our hero into that territory, it will be well to take a panoramic view of the vast wilderness west of the stately mountains which tower above the rippling waters of the Watauga, and to take a look at its early dwellers.

Standing on these lofty mountain heights, the explorer might have beheld a wide expanse of forest, a forest clothing one of the richest and most beautiful spots on the face of the earth. In the distance vast herds of buffaloes grazed, bear lurked in the dense cane-brake, and deer fled over the hills. By day, the wilderness was flooded with the music of countless song-birds; by night, the solitude was broken by the howls of wolves, the screams of panthers, and the hoots of horn-owls. This wild but beautiful country was the inter-tribal park and hunting-ground of the Red Man of the forest. Living among these mountains as the Cherokee did, we do not wonder that he left us so many poetical names. Think of the sweetness of sound in the name *Watauga*.

The taste and disposition of the Indians differed from those of the white men. They were naturally very fond of athletic games;[1] they enjoyed foot-racing and wrestling, and dancing was a favorite pastime. The war-dance was usually indulged in before going upon the war-path. One of their most popular games was played with balls and rackets, somewhat like the modern game of lacrosse. The ball, usually about the size of a baseball, was made of deer-skin, stuffed hard with hair. This ball was knocked by rackets made of sticks about two feet long, strung with raw-hide. The game was sometimes played by select players, but often by all the young men of a village. One village frequently played against another, or one tribe strove for the championship against another tribe. When they came together at the appointed time and place, every player arrayed in his best, they found great crowds of spectators assembled to see the contest. All things being ready, the game was ushered in by solemn dances and religious ceremonies. During the game a successful hit was followed by loud applause from the enthusiastic crowd. The excited players often rushed together in a scrimmage, each side eager to win, and one or two players came out of the contest with broken bones. All these games and sports helped to develop the fine physique of the Indian warrior.

Many tribes claimed access to the common hunting-ground, but no tribe dared to make a home within its boundaries, lest the other tribes combine for its complete extermination. The particular tribes claiming an interest in the coveted hunting-ground were the Creek, the Chickasaw, the Uchee, the Shawnee, the Chickamauga, and the Cherokee. The last two most directly concern us at present.

In order to appreciate the peculiar difficulties which confronted the white man in his attempts to settle in this wilderness, we shall have to understand the fiery, martial spirit of the Cherokees especially. Their tribal name is derived from *Cheera*, which means fire, and fire is regarded their lower heaven. They call their medicine men Cheera-tahge, or the men possessed of divine fire. Forty years before the breaking out of the Revolutionary war, this powerful tribe had, it is said, sixty-four towns; and old traders estimated the number of their warriors to be above six thousand. They liked war and were not content unless engaged in martial conflicts. In reply to an earnest appeal of the white people, that they

[1] Bartram, Adair.

establish peace between themselves and the Tuscaroras, they said: "We cannot live without war. Should we make peace with the Tuscaroras, we must immediately look out for some other, with whom we can be engaged in our beloved occupation." They loved a brave man and despised a coward. Speaking of the Indian's passion for revenge, one writer has said: "I have known them to go a thousand miles for the purpose of revenge, in pathless woods, over hills and mountains, through large cane-swamps full of grape-vines and briars, over broad lakes, rapid rivers, and deep creeks; all the way endangered by poisonous snakes, if not with the rambling and lurking enemy; while, at the same time, they were exposed to the extremities of heat and cold, the vicissitudes of the seasons, to hunger and thirst . . . to fatigues and other difficulties. Such is their over-boiling revengeful temper, that they utterly contemn all those as imaginary trifles, if they are so happy as to get the scalps of the murderer or enemy, to satisfy the supposed craving ghost of their deceased relations."[2] These characteristics, existing to a more or less degree in all Indians, were fully developed in the Cherokee and the Chickamauga. Intellectually, the Cherokee tribe was among the strongest of American tribes. We shall learn more of this tribe, and find that John Sevier was perhaps the only man on the frontier who could outgeneral its cunning warriors.

The English pushed into this romantic region, and established Fort Loudon in 1756. This region was included in the grant which Charles II made in 1663 to a company of men called Lords Proprietors, the grant including the country between the present States of Virginia and Florida, and extending from the Atlantic to the Pacific ocean. A small settlement sprang up under the protection of this fort, but the old fort has a sad story to tell.

The Cherokees assisted the English in their second expedition against the French at Fort Duquesne, which brought victory and peace to the English, gaining for the crown of Great Britain the Ohio country and all the territory south to the Gulf of Mexico and east of the Mississippi River, except the Isle Orleans. The Indian warriors had lost many of their horses in this expedition, and, as they were returning to their homes, they caught some horses running at large in Virginia. The Virginians became offended at the Indians and killed some of their warriors, and then the Cherokee warriors, of course, desired revenge. Gathering together a large band of warriors, they took the war-path and in 1758 laid siege to Fort Loudon under the command of Captains Demere and Stuart. The whites sent out for help, but their messengers were murdered by the Indians. A few friendly squaws stole in by a secret passage at night with a small supply of beans, but this was not sufficient to satisfy their hunger, and the starving inmates fell to eating the flesh of their horses and dogs. Finally Captain Stuart went to Chota to ask for terms. It was agreed that the whites should abandon the fort, with its guns and powder, and return to their homes in Virginia and North Carolina. They had the promise of a safe passage through the Indian country under the protection of an escort of Indian warriors. They encamped the night after their departure near an Indian village on the Tellico plains. The next morning about daylight a band of infuriated Cherokees fell upon them, and few were left to tell the mournful story of the massacre that ensued. It is said that the Indians afterwards made a fence of the bones of the dead white men left upon the plains after this terrible massacre.

From this time on, the Indians were very jealous of the encroachments of the white men upon their lands, but traders continued to traffic with them, and hunters and trappers frequently crossed over the mountains, exploring and hunting in the new country. Returning to the East, they fascinated their neighbors with glowing descriptions of the magnificent region. Daniel Boone, the celebrated hunter and explorer, was among the first to explore and hunt in these western wilds. It is said that while standing on the summit of the Alleghanies, facing the beautiful region into which he was about to enter, he exclaimed to his companion: "I am richer than the man in Scripture who owned the cattle on a thou-
[2] Adair.

sand hills. I own the wild beasts of a thousand valleys."

Boone pushed on into the unexplored wilderness, hunting the wild beasts with his flint-lock rifle. He caused the light of his bravery and invincible spirit of adventure to illuminate the pathway of the pioneer when he took his hunting-knife and carved on a large beech-tree standing on the bank of Boone's Creek the inscription: " D Boon Cilled A Bar On Tree in The yEar 1760."

Story after story about the new country was related till it became common talk in the towns along the Atlantic. After the French and Indian War, a few people, impelled by British tyranny and allured by hopes of obtaining better lands and more independence, made up their minds to move into the new country. The French had told the Indians that the English, if victorious in gaining possession of the territory claimed by France, would take their lands from them and deprive them of their hunting-grounds. So, when the French were defeated, the Indians believed that the English would next fall upon them and seize their hunting-grounds. To quiet their apprehensions, George III of England issued a proclamation in 1763 prohibiting any private purchase of land by any citizen or any grant of lands, by any governor, west of the sources of the streams which flow into the Atlantic. He also said that none of his subjects should make settlements on individual lands west of the sources of these streams.

This order of the king prevented many people from settling in the fertile region explored by Boone and his companions, but the thrilling stories stirred the adventurous spirit of a few pioneers who were willing to risk the king's displeasure. So they crossed the mountains and made their settlements, claiming, as an excuse for violating the proclamation, the treaty of Fort Stanwix, a treaty made in October, 1767, which fixed a boundary line for the Indians of the Six Nations and conceded to the British the whole country south of the Ohio River.

The physical formation of this beautiful region was very favorable for an inflow of immigration. It was as if some Titanic power had plowed a deep furrow in the middle of the great Alleghanies, forming the beautiful long valley extending from Virginia into the picturesque region explored by Boone and others. Along this valley ran the old war-path of the various Indian tribes. It was an inviting pathway to the Southwest, and it received the impress of some of the best families of Virginia.

The North Holston Settlement was founded in what is now Sullivan County, Tennessee. The leading family in it was the Shelbys. General Evan Shelby, who settled at Meadows, was a noted Indian fighter, and his son, Colonel Isaac Shelby, later fought heroically in the battle of King's Mountain. In Tennessee the family name is preserved in Shelby County, in the southwestern part of the State, and in the town of Shelbyville, the county-seat of Bedford County, near the center of the State. The Carter's Valley Settlement, made about 1770, was in what is now Hawkins County, Tennessee, and was a part of the Virginia settlement which had been extended down from Wolf Hills.

The most noted of the four western settlements was the one made at Watauga, on the Watauga River, near the present Elizabethton, Tennessee. The first settler was William Bean, a bold hunter from Virginia, who had previously hunted with Boone in this region. Their old camping-ground was on Boone's Creek, a tributary of Watauga River, not very far from that river, and in 1769 Bean built his hut on the very spot where he and Boone had previously camped together. There in that lonely cabin his son, Russell Bean, was born, the first white child born in what is now the State of Tennessee. Other people, from Virginia, settled near Bean's cabin; and, soon afterwards, came many settlers from Wake County, North Carolina, in search of homes, many of whom, as soldiers, had seen the rich country as they went to the relief of Fort Loudon in 1758.

An important event in the early days of Watauga was the arrival of James Robertson in the spring of 1770. Though he came from North Carolina, he was a native of Brunswick County, Virginia. He was taciturn and thoughtful, and in every way a man well suited to the trying position which he was about to assume. He was hospitably entertained by a hunter and recent settler at Watauga named Honeycut and by William Bean. Deciding at once to make his home at Watauga, he selected and cleared a spot of ground and planted and raised a crop of corn.

After harvesting his first crop of corn, Robertson set out for North Carolina for his family and a few neighbors who were desirous of moving to the new settlements. On recrossing the mountains, he got lost. Wandering about for some time, he came to a cliff where he had to leave his horse. Heavy showers fell and drenched his powder so that he could not kill any game for food. For fourteen days he trudged about in the mountains without anything to eat, except a few nuts and berries, and became so weak that he despaired of ever reaching his home again. Accidentally two hunters chanced to find him. They gave him food, furnished him a horse to ride, and soon he returned to Watauga with his family and the neighbors he had guided to their new homes.

British aggression in the colonies since the French and Indian war had been arousing the spirit of independence and resistance and now gave a new impulse to immigration into this region from North Carolina. In 1771 this impetus was strengthened by the defeat of the popular uprising in the eastern colonies. The Regulators, citizens banded together to resist the imposition of taxes by England, and the efforts of Governor Tryon to impose other taxes for the building of an executive mansion, were defeated in the battle of Alamance on the 16th of May and forced into retreat before the royal troops. They were not cowed by their defeat, however, these North Carolinians; "like the mammoth, they shook the bolt from their brow and crossed the mountain" and were received with gladness by the settlers at Watauga. With this voluntary exile to the western wilds began the exodus from North Carolina which swelled the population of the little settlement, and gave the Wataugans a prominent place in history.

In 1772 Jacob Brown settled on the north bank of the Nolichucky River, founding the second south Holston, or

Nolichucky Settlement, which was one of the most noted of the western settlements. By the Indians the river was called *Nonachunheh*, which means rapid or precipitous. This beautiful river rises high up in the Alleghanies and flows down the mountain side through scenery beautiful beyond description. Brown was a merchant, and in exchange for the small store of goods brought with him on a single packhorse, he secured the lease of a large tract of land from the Cherokees. He afterwards leased portions of his land to other settlers, thus making considerable profits.

The persecuted people living on the Atlantic seaboard were glad to find such a retreat, and the settlements were thronged with people of the best blood of North Carolina and Virginia. Here they felt secure from the oppression of the colonial government. Living in the shadow of the Alleghanies as they did, we do not wonder that the love of freedom swelled every man's bosom; and it is not surprising to see them rise up from their mountain homes, like the Swiss, when the time came to strike a blow for freedom and independence.

CHAPTER THREE

The Watauga Association

Anglo-Saxons have always been characterized by a love of law and order and free institutions. The settlements on the banks of the Watauga lay in the red man's Garden of Eden, and peace and friendship prevailed in every cabin till fugitives from justice crept into the new settlements, fugitives from the States along the Atlantic. Then the settlers felt the need of a fixed system of government, by which violations of the law could be punished. They were too far back in the wilderness to be under the immediate protection of either North Carolina or Virginia, and, as they could not live peaceably and prosperously without courts to regulate their affairs, the demands of the people became greater with the rapid increase of population.

Imagine the critical condition of these settlements. When they first settled on the banks of the Watauga, they thought they were within the bounds of Virginia; but, in 1771, the boundary line between North Carolina and Virginia was surveyed from Steep Rock to Beaver Creek, and, much to the disappointment of the Wataugans, it was discovered that the settlements were in North Carolina. Virginia at once made a treaty with the Cherokees, making the boundary line of their lands identical with the new State line. The settlers could no longer rely upon Virginia for protection; they were beyond reach of the authority of North Carolina and living on Indian lands controlled by the King of England; the King's proclamation forbade their purchasing an of the land upon which they had built their cabins and lawless bands of fugitives and outlaws from the seaboard annoyed them day and night. The whole situation was distressing in the extreme, and the prospects became still more gloomy, when, in the spring of 1772, Alexander Cameron, British Agent of the Southern Indians, warned the settlers off the Indian lands.

Fortunately, the Cherokees had been engaged in war with the Creeks and Chickasaws so incessantly that their ranks were thinned and their martial spirits quieted for a time. Having been terribly beaten by the Chickasaws, they were in a state of mind to be friendly toward the settlers, and they even expressed a desire that the settlers be allowed to remain in their new homes, provided, of course, they would not make any further encroachments.

This act of kindness on the part of the Cherokees gave some relief to the settlers, who were determined to remain in their cabins, for the hardships of the frontier-life did not affect them as much as the acts of the English authorities east of the Alleghanies. Finally they decided to form a free government of their own, and in 1772 came together to try their hands at commonwealth building. The meeting was held at Watauga. They drew; up and adopted the "Articles of the Watauga Association," and formed the first written constitution ever adopted by American-born freemen. They incorporated such of the laws of Virginia as they deemed sufficient to carry on their little commonwealth successfully, and every man in the little settlement signed the constitution. A committee of thirteen was elected to make such additional laws as the welfare of the settlement required. This committee appointed five commissioners from their own number to settle disputes, punish offenders, and perform the legal business common to the courts. Thus law and order were established, and the people began to prosper under their free government. A whipping-post was established for the punishment of offenders, and graver offenses were punished by hanging. As an example of the prompt action and unfaltering determination of these pioneers in putting down crime, we find on record the case of a horse-thief, who was captured on Monday, given a fair trial on Wednesday, and hanged on Friday of the same week. It is to be regretted that the articles of this association have not been preserved. Doctor Ramsey claims that John Sevier was elected by the Watauga settlers as one of the thirteen commissioners, he believes, also, that Sevier was chosen as one of the committee of five to act as a court.[1] It is true that Sevier was at Watauga in 1772 the year the Watauga Association was formed, but it seems rather strange that they should choose him, as he was a stranger and there on an exploring trip only. As Sevier did not move into these settlements until December 25, 1773, he certainly was not in a position to render the Association any service for more than a year.

The people next turned their attention to the question of leasing land from the Indians. The king's proclamation prevented the purchase of land, but the pioneers reasoned that if they only leased the lands for a specific period of time that would not be in violation of the king's proclamation and would suit them much better than returning to the unhappy conditions in the States which they had just left. John Boone and James Robertson were selected by the settlers to negotiate with the Indians. Many of the chiefs and warriors assembled near Watauga and leased to the white men for ten years all the lands on the waters of the Watauga, the Indians receiving for the lease five or six thousand dollars' worth of merchandise, including a few muskets.

In the midst of the celebration which followed the successful negotiation of the lease, there was an important occurrence that came near being attended with serious consequences. Some lawless intruders upon the settlements, men from Wolf Hills, Virginia, it is supposed, killed one of the Indians who was taking part in the sports held in celebration of the cordial relations established between the Indians and the white men. To the Cherokees this seemed a serious breach of faith. All their war spirit was aroused. To the great alarm of the settlers, they immediately left the settlement with the merchandise assigned to them as consideration for their lease, and showed every sign of seeking revenge for the affront that had been offered them in the slaying of one of their number.

The occasion demanding immediate action on the part of the settlers, James Robertson went to the Indian towns a distance of one hundred and fifty miles, in order to pacify the warriors and again secure their friendship. Explaining to the head-men that the crime was committed by an outlaw from Virginia, and that the Wataugans intended to punish the culprit if they could lay hands on him, the chiefs and warriors were satisfied and were again ready to smoke the pipe of peace with their white brother. The journey was an extremely hazardous one, but the safety of the settlements demanded it. Robertson was, therefore, ever afterwards held in especial esteem for the noble service to his fellow-settlers.

Sevier's life as a small merchant at New Market and subsequently at Millerstown was rather too monotonous for his active, restless nature, and he longed for more stirring scenes. He had listened eagerly to the stories of the adventurers and settlers on the Holston and the Watauga, he had heard much of the rich soil of the well-watered region, and he longed to visit the new settlements. So, arming himself and mounting his favorite horse, he took leave of his family at Millerstown and went out to Holston River in 1771 on an exploring trip, passing the mouth of the Watauga River.[2] He was so delighted with the country, the wild game, and the rich soil that he came again in 1772. This time he visited the settlers at Watauga, probably about the time of the establishment of the Watauga Association, and formed a life-long friendship with Robertson, Bean, Honeycut, and others of like prominence in the settlement.

Having thus seen much of the frontier, Sevier decided to settle at Holston, as that settlement seemed to present the most favorable prospects. He built his cabin about one mile north of the Holston River and returned to Virginia for his family. He carried the news of his plan to his father and

[1] Ramsey's "Annals of Tennessee," p. 107

mother and brothers and sisters, and all, without hesitation, decided to move into the same country with him. It is quite probable that John's brother, Valentine, was with him on the former's first exploring trip, as he was the first of the Sevier family to move to the new settlements, having moved there with his family in 1772.

In December, 1773, John Sevier, with his own family, his parents, his three brothers, Robert, Joseph, and Abraham—Valentine having preceded them—and his two sisters, Polly and Catherine, took his departure from his Virginia home, from the hills and valleys where the happiest part of his youth was spent, and began the slow, fatiguing journey towards his new home. He had certainly not lost his interest in the mercantile business, for he brought with him a store of goods on pack-horses.

On Christmas day, 1773, the Seviers came to the end of their journey, and each family went to its own cabin. Sevier's parents finally settled upon a rich tract of land near Watauga. His father's subsequent life was one of great industry and influence. He lived to the ripe old age of one hundred years, dying in Carter's City on Friday, December 30, 1803.[3]

It has been a subject of speculation as to Sevier's motive in removing to these extreme frontier settlements. He had explored the country before deciding to remove, and no doubt foresaw the possibilities in the development of the great Southwest. He felt too, perhaps, that there was promise of feature distinction for him in the new country.

A look into those western settlements will show us many strange sights. The people were hardy, resolute, fearless; they expected to face dangers and endure hardships. The cabins were very rude in appearance, comfort being the chief aim of the builders. Built of logs cut from the forests, these cabins were made strong to resist the sieges of the Indians, having port-holes through which the occupants could aim their flint-locks in case of an attack. The planks for the doors and floors were hewn with the broad-ax, the windows had no glass and were fitted with wooden shutters, the chimney was

[2] Draper MSS.

naturally "stick and dirt," but was sometimes built of rough stone, and the fire-place was wide and held a great quantity of wood. Most of the furniture was home-made, but sometimes a chair, table, or stool imported from England was brought into the settlement. Every household had a spinning-wheel and a loom which the women used very skillfully in the manufacture of cloth. At night the cabin was lighted by the candle. The men, returning from the fields or from the hunt, tired and hungry, ate with thankful hearts the plain healthful meals set before them. After supper, the family spent the first hours of the night in conversation and story-telling. Sometimes, during the autumn months, they spent the hours profitably by spinning thread, weaving cloth, and making shoes to keep themselves comfortable during the winter. If there were no other amusements for the children, the grandfather or grandmother narrated interesting stories to them till bed-time.

The people were cheerful. The brisk, pure air was Nature's tonic and they partook freely. Their social gatherings kept them in a pleasant humor towards each other. The men and boys delighted in shooting-matches, corn-huskings, horse-races, bear-hunts, and deer-drives; the women often came together at quilting bees and spent many a pleasant hour together. Occasionally the young people met at night in social gatherings and enjoyed their games and sports, sometimes dancing to the music of the fiddle.

Their style of dress is interesting. The men and boys wore short pantaloons, leather leggings reaching above the knees, and the famous hunting-shirts. These hunting-shirts, made sometimes of heavy cloth, but usually of deer-skin, were worn over the other clothing. They were cut and made like ordinary shirts, but were open their entire length, and were girt with belts, in which were carried the hunting-knife and the tomahawk.

On his first appearance among the settlers of North Holston and Watauga, Sevier attracted considerable attention on account of his handsome face, manly bearing and remark-

[3] Draper MSS.

ably winning manners. No man ever had a more symmetrical, well-knit frame. He was five feet nine inches in height and weighed one hundred and ninety pounds.[4] His complexion was ruddy, indicating his perfect health; he had small, keen, dark-blue eyes, expressive of vivacity and fearlessness; his nose was prominent; his mouth and chin, the model of firmness; his hair, fair, and his face was expressive of sympathy for humanity. His wonderful personal magnetism attracted the friendship of all.

Immigration continued to pour into the new settlements, and business among the settlers gradually increased, and Sevier's little store helped to supply the people with goods. The peltries he bartered were sent on packhorses to eastern markets and exchanged for goods for his store. He was scarcely settled in his mercantile business, however, when in 1774 a quarrel arose between Lord Dunmore and the Shawnees. Thus far Sevier had not distinguished himself as a warrior among the western settlers. He was better known as a useful citizen and business man, but his fame as an Indian fighter in his younger days on the Virginia frontiers had doubtless reached the Wataugans. Indeed he was not unknown to Lord Dunmore, the royal governor of Virginia, who was so impressed with his bravery that he appointed him captain in the Virginia line, at the outbreak of the war with the Shawnees.

CHAPTER FOUR

The Fighting Heroes of Watauga

The battle of the great Kanawha, fought October 10th 1774, was one of the most sanguinary and hotly contested battles in the annals of Indian warfare; and it is especially interesting to us because in it the Wataugans first showed to the world their wonderful skill in battle.

The Shawnees, becoming greatly enraged at the surveyors sent out from Virginia to mark out lands given under royal grants and military warrants, murdered several of them. Lord Dunmore, the royal governor of Virginia, at once declared war against the Shawnees. Hence the war is sometimes known as Lord Dunmore's War.

Open hostilities had already begun in October, 1773, when a war-party of Indians attacked Boone and his companions, who were enroute to Kentucky in search of homes. Before this time no women and children of the white race had ever crossed the Cumberland Mountains. Boone had induced several families to join in the journey with him and his family, and the party was moving on slowly towards the Cumberland Gap. When they reached Powell's Valley, they were joined by forty bold hunters. The company, now eighty in all, moved onward, wending their way through the rugged mountain passes with a feeling of greater safety, but on October 5th, while passing through a narrow, rocky defile, they were assaulted by a band of Indians lying in ambush. At the

⁴ Draper MSS.

flash of the Indians' first fire, six white men fell and a seventh was wounded. Among the killed was a son of Boone, about twenty years of age. Some of the hunters hurried to the rescue of the women and children; the others quickly put the Indians to flight. Boone and his party then fell back to Watauga, where they remained till the close of the war. They then pushed on into Kentucky and made their settlements.

Almost daily deeds of violence were committed. Murder followed murder, and doubtless wrongs were committed on both sides, through misunderstandings or otherwise. Butler, a trader with the Indians, was robbed of his peltries by the Cherokees. He sent two friendly Shawnees to recover his peltries, but they were ambushed and killed by white men, probably through a mistake, an outrage which met with the severest disapproval of the better class of pioneers.

A party of Indians, including the family of Logan, a famous Iroquois warrior and chief, noted especially for his friendliness to the white men, crossed the river on a visit to Mr. Greathouse. The simple-minded savages were intoxicated with liquor and massacred by Greathouse and others. The unfortunate Logan, manly and dignified in appearance, was a noted hunter and a skillful marksman. On his face was stamped nobility of character. He was declared by one white hunter to be the best specimen of humanity he ever met with, either white or red. But the murder of his kinsmen aroused the rage of Logan, and led him to relinquish all love and friendship for the white men, and to do all he could to destroy them.

The acts committed against the Indians by a few unprincipled white men were often unjust, but the Indians committed graver crimes by murdering helpless women and children, and certainly deserved the fate they met in Dunmore's War. Several other tribes joined the Shawnees in their awful deeds of slaughter, and the war extended the length of the frontier. The pioneers rushed eagerly to Dunmore's army for the protection of their homes.

The army of the white men marched in two wings, the right wing being commanded by Dunmore himself, and the left by General Andrew Lewis. The two wings were to unite at the mouth of the Great Kanawha River.

Dunmore led his wing to Fort Pitt, where he foolishly changed his plans, abandoning the scheme agreed upon by him and Lewis, and took his army down the Ohio in boats and canoes to the mouth of the Hockhocking. Thence he went to the Scioto and fortified himself. Lewis met his men at the levels of the Greenbrier. Each had done what he could in this hasty preparation for war.

Impatient for action, General Lewis did not wait for all his men to arrive, but marched on to the mouth of Elk Creek, which empties into the Great Kanawha, and set to work making dug-out canoes to descend that river.

Meanwhile John Sevier had not been idle. He was one of the most active in raising men, provisions, arms, and ammunition for the war, but he thought it wise to remain at Watauga to defend the settlers against any Indian attack that might be made in the absence of the volunteers. Captain Shelby commanded the company of fifty or more brave men, among whom was Valentine Sevier, raised at Watauga. He joined the regiment of Colonel Christian on New River; and out traveling the regiment, hastened on with his company to the army of General Lewis on the Great Kanawha.

By the first of October, the army of General Lewis began to move down the river. A part of the soldiers descended the river in canoes, while the other division went by land, all reaching the mouth of the river on the 6th of October. Though in good spirits and anxious for battle, some of the soldiers were not satisfied with their rations, claiming that favoritism was shown in the issue of beef; and select parties of hunters went into the woods each day to kill game for meat.

Affairs in camp went on well for awhile, but, on the 9th, Simon Girty arrived with a message from Dunmore, ordering Lewis to break up camp and join him near Pickaway Plains. General Lewis was not pleased with the change, but decided to comply with the order next morning. That night, while the soldiers slept, the old Shawnee Chief, Cornstalk, was busy ferrying his men over the river on rafts some six or eight miles above them, coming to make an attack upon Lewis.

On the morning of the 10th small parties went out to hunt game for breakfast, and two men from Russell's company, breasting the woods not far apart, came suddenly upon Corn-stalk's warriors, nearly a thousand strong, marching in the direction of the camp of General Lewis. Russell's men saw the warriors first and fired. The Indians returned the fire, killing one of the men. The other man ran into the camp. The echo of the first fire had scarcely died away when Valentine Sevier and James Robertson also fired and fled to camp, reaching it about as soon as the other refugee.

Drum-beats aroused the slumbering soldiers. Two detachments, under command of Colonel Charles Lewis and Colonel William Fleming, were ordered out to check the advancing foe. The two armies met in the dense forest about sunrise, and battle ensued. The wild war-whoops of the Indians and the sharp cracks of the pioneers' rifles filled the brisk morning air with a deafening noise which convinced General Lewis that a strong force of the enemy was at hand. He, therefore, hurried Colonel Fields, with two hundred men, into the battle.

The contest lasted all day; all day the armies surged to and fro, the grim-visaged warriors yelling themselves hoarse. The situation taxed the genius of General Lewis, and the chance of victory seemed uncertain. In the afternoon he ordered Captains Shelby, Stewart, and Matthews to move their companies up the Kanawha and fire upon the Indians from the rear. As they were passing along the bank of the river, they were fired upon by some Indians concealed behind a breast-work of logs and brush. The passage was difficult on account of the withering fire from the ambush, but John Sawyer, one of Shelby's men, took a few riflemen and made a gallant charge upon the Indians. The warriors fled, and three pioneer companies gained the rear and poured a shower of lead into the ranks of the Indians, forcing them into a hasty retreat. Again they halted in another position, sheltered by a dense undergrowth, and kept up an occasional firing till nightfall, when they recrossed the river and hastened to their towns on the Scioto.

Thus ended the bloody battle. The Wataugans had behaved themselves well in the whole engagement. It was their vigilance that discovered the advancing enemy and sounded the alarm of danger, and it was the gallant charge of Shelby's men that turned the tide of battle and brought victory to the white men.

Peace was established with the Shawnees, but the brave Logan was absent from the council at which the pipe of peace was smoked. He was so hurt over the murder of his family and kin that he did not feel disposed to attend, but he sent the following pathetic, yet truly eloquent, message on paper to Lord Dunmore:

"I appeal to any white man to say, if ever he entered Logan's cabin hungry and he gave him not meat; if ever he came cold and naked and he clothed him not? During the course of the last long and bloody war, Logan remained idle in his camp, an advocate for peace. Such was my love for the whites that my countrymen pointed as I passed and said, 'Logan is the friend of the white man.' I had even thought to have lived with you but for the injuries of one man, Colonel Cresap, the last spring, in cold blood and unprovoked, murdered all the relations of Logan, not even sparing my women and children. There runs not a drop of my blood in the veins of any living creature. This called on me for revenge. I have sought it. I have killed many. I have fully glutted my vengeance. For my country I rejoice at the beams of peace; but do not harbor a thought that mine is the joy of fear. Logan never felt fear. He will not turn on his heel to save his life. Who is there to mourn for Logan? Not one."[1]

The Wataugans returned to their homes and resumed their occupations. Having fought heroically, they now rejoiced over the victory and many a household was stirred by the thrilling stories of the Kanawha.

The affairs in the settlements went on successfully. The population continued to increase, and the little cabins were hives of industry. No drones were permitted among them, and for a while after the battle of Kanawha the settlers followed their pursuits in peace. But again the dark clouds of war began to rise in the East, and the affairs of the Wataugans were again disturbed. The powder-horn and the flint-lock rifle were again taken from the rack; the sword again drawn from the scabbard; and the drum-beats for war were heard. And every man of Anglo-Saxon blood, born with the love of freedom and unwilling to be fettered with the chain of British tyranny, felt in every fiber the wrong done him by the English king.

Within a little more than a century, twenty-five Navigation Acts, acts unjust to the American colonists, had been passed by the British Parliament. The Colonists were compelled to ship their goods in English vessels to English ports, and as this gave the English the monopoly of the American trade, the Colonists soon became resentful of such unjust legislation. Consequently smuggling became so prevalent in New England that "Writs of Assistance" were issued by the courts of the king, giving revenue officers the right to enter warehouses and dwellings in search of smuggled goods.

The continued slave-trade in the colonies carried on entirely by England was a grievous annoyance to every loyal American. The treaty of Utrecht, in 1713, gave England entire control of the American slave-trade; as it was a profitable business, she would not allow any laws to go into effect which were made by her subjects to prohibit the importation of slaves. The troubles with the Indians had been caused by England's bad management or entire neglect. The inter-colonial wars had heaped a heavy debt upon the Crown, and now Parliament passed the Stamp Act with the intention of forcing the Colonists to help lift the debt, claiming as their justification that the Colonists reaped benefits from the wars.

Opposition to British aggression arose on every side, and remonstrances were heard from every quarter. Everywhere the trumpet blasts of the Revolution were sounded by noble

[1] "The Winning of the West," Vol. I.

patriots.

"English people cannot be taxed," said Judge Drayton of South Carolina in charging a grand-jury, "nay, they cannot be bound by any law, unless by their consent, expressed by themselves or by the representatives of their own election. I charge you to do your duty; to maintain the laws, the rights, the constitution of your own country, even at the hazard of your lives and fortunes. In my judicial character I know no law, I am a servant, not to the king, but to the constitution."

Doctor Warren, one of the earliest martyrs to the cause of liberty, said: "It is the united voice of America to preserve their freedom or lose their lives in the defense of it. Their resolutions are not the effects of inconsiderate rashness, but the sound result of sober inquiry and deliberation. I am convinced that the true spirit of liberty was never so universally diffused through all ranks and orders of people in any country on the face of the earth, as it now is through all North America."

Patrick Henry, as he stood before the Virginia Convention, assembled in St. John's Episcopal Church, Richmond, sounded the voice of prophecy when he said, "The next gale that sweeps from the North will bring to our ears the clash of resounding arms."

That prophecy was fulfilled when, on the 19th of April, 1775, at Concord and Lexington, Massachusetts, "the embattled farmers stood, and fired the shot heard round the world." The Revolution had begun. Patriots throughout the colonies enlisted in their country's cause. The Continental Congress proceeded to place the colonies upon a war basis, and, by the election of General George Washington as commander-in-chief of their armies, gave definite form and organization to their resistance to British aggression.

The patriots in North Carolina were neither listless nor idle. As we have seen, the Regulators had resisted the aggressions of Governor Tryon; and, in the May following the battles of Concord and Lexington, and before the battle of Bunker Hill, the people of Mecklenburg County, North Carolina, meeting at Charlotte, the county seat, adopted certain resolutions which were a vigorous protest against the British colonial policy as exhibited in North Carolina, and which were couched in language subsequently claimed to have been the original of the famous Declaration of Independence.[2]

As has been already noted, British aggressions in North Carolina had stimulated emigration to the settlements west of the mountains. A sturdy class of patriots, men who preferred the hardships of the wilderness and perils from the Indians to the sacrifice of their freedom in the more favored eastern country, moved to the new settlements. They built their cabins in the shadows of the great mountains along the Holston, the Watauga, and the Nolichucky, hoping that they would be able to enjoy the freedom which is the inheritance of every Anglo-Saxon.

But the Wataugans had no intention of enjoying their safety in their secluded frontier homes regardless of the dangers encountered by the Americans on the seaboard. They fully recognized their close relationship to the patriots of the colonies, and, when the first clash of arms was heard from the North, they espoused the cause of liberty and showed their sympathy with that cause by naming their country Washington District, in honor of the new commander-in-chief. Their population had grown to nearly six hundred, and they began to feel strong enough to render assistance to the common cause. In order to put themselves in a position to render greater service to their country, they appealed to North Carolina for recognition. The petition proved successful; in the following year, Washington District became Washington County, and the laws of North Carolina were extended to its courts.

John Sevier, who had already won the esteem and respect of his neighbors, and two other citizens from Watauga were chosen as delegates to the Constitutional Convention which met at Halifax, North Carolina, November 12, 1776. In the Declaration of Rights adopted by the Convention, we find, in the clause defining the State limits, this sentence: "That it shall not be so construed as to prevent the establishment of one or more governments westward of this State, by consent of the Legislature." This clause, introduced by Sevier himself, shows clearly that he was thus early musing a project for founding a commonwealth in the great Mississippi Valley.

[2] The present writer has no intention of taking either side in the controversy which has long been waged over the so-called "Mecklenburg Declaration of Independence." Any discussion of the subject would be out of place here. The reference is given solely to show the temper of the North Carolinians at that time.

CHAPTER V

Indian Disturbances

The British Superintendent of Southern Indian Affairs at this time was John Stuart, a man well aware of the opposition to British aggressions developing in the Watauga settlements and of the activity of the Wataugans in their preparations for resistance. To defeat these preparations, he conceived a plan for a simultaneous attack of the British and the Indians upon the Americans. According to this plan, Sir Peter Parker was to capture Charleston, South Carolina, with the king's fleet, and land an army here under Sir Henry Clinton, to sweep everything along the coast, while the Indians were to fall upon the frontier settlements. The plan was laid before the British Cabinet and was adopted by the British Parliament despite the opposition of Lord Chatham. Alexander Cameron, a Scotchman, and a subordinate of John Stuart, was sent among the Indians with such merchandise and trinkets as would appeal to them in order to gain their sympathy and support.

News of the British war-plan reached the ears of Nancy Ward, a Cherokee squaw, who was well known to the settlers, and whose home was at Echota, the chief village of the Cherokees. This woman was the prophetess of the Cherokees, but she always had a kindly feeling for the white people and befriended them in every way she could. Her father was an English officer, and her mother was a sister of the Indian chief, Atta-culla-culla. She sent news of the intended attack to the white men by her old friend Isaac Thomas, a trader, and the settlers made hasty preparation for defense.

Though most of the western settlers were Whigs, patriots espousing the cause of the colonists, it was rumored among the Wat+augans that several Tories, as those in sympathy with the British were called, were living at Nolichucky. Without delay a large number of men from Holston, Carter's Valley, and Watauga went to Brown's store and forced the suspected Tories to take the oath of allegiance to the common cause. About this time the murder of Boyd and Dogget, two traders who were returning from the Indian villages, served to inflame the people still more and to hurry their defensive measures to completion. Several forts were built, and the people hurried into them for safety. Everything in the Indian villages was astir with the preparations for war. War-belts were received from other tribes, and a concerted movement was developing rapidly. Early in July, 1776 messengers brought to the Wat+augans tidings of the Indians' approach. John Sevier at once sent the following message to the Virginia Committee:

Fort Lee, July 11, 1776.

Dear Gentlemen: Isaac Thomas, William Falling, Jaret Williams, and one more, have this moment come in by making their escape from the Indians, and say six hundred Indians and whites were to start for this fort, and intend to drive the country up to New River before they return.

John Sevier

The news of the intended invasion had been imparted to Isaac Thomas by Nancy Ward by night. Thomas in turn gave the information to Falling and Williams and the other messenger, and they all set out for Watauga, each by a different route to make sure the delivery of the message. The other settlements were informed of the coming danger. Spies and scouts were kept in the woods to watch for the Indians. The attack was to be made all along the frontiers of the southern colonies. The Creeks were to fall upon Georgia; the Shawnees, Mingoes, and Delawares, upon Virginia; and seven hundred Cherokees and Chickamaugas, upon the Watauga settlements. The Cherokees were to advance upon the settlers in two divisions of equal numbers, to be commanded respectively by Old Abraham and Dragging Canoe. Old Abraham of Chilhowee was to march along the foot of the mountains and attack Watauga; Dragging Canoe was to march upon Fort Heaton, which was between the north and south branches of the Holston River, about six miles from where they unite; and, after the destruction of these forts, they were to invade the western settlements of Virginia.

In answer to Sevier's message, five small companies, made up largely of Virginians, reached Fort Heaton, where they remained two or three days to protect the people and to find out, if possible, the designs of the Indians. The corps in the fort consisted of one hundred and seventy men, a very small army to resist the vast Indian forces.

At last the scouts returned from the woods with tidings that the Indians were near and that they were marching directly upon Fort Heaton. A council was held to determine whether to wait in the fort for the Indians to make the attack or to march out and meet them in the woods. Some of the garrison preferred to wait for them, but Captain Cocke argued that the Indians would not attack the fort, but would fall upon the settlements in small parties and murder helpless women and children who had not reached the fort. His argument having prevailed, the little army marched out towards Island Flats in two divisions, flankers on each side and scouts in front.

The advance-guard of about twelve men met a small band of Indians on Island Flats and fired upon them. The Indians returned the fire, but the fire from the white men forced them to flee. Anticipating a large force of Indians near at hand, a halt was made, and as night was coming on, it was decided best to return to the fort. Before the soldiers had gone very far, the Indians rushed upon their rear, amid the din of war-whoops, yelling to their comrades, "The Unacas are running! Come on and scalp them!" Captain Thomas, the chief officer, heading the left line, ordered the right and left lines to face the enemy for battle, and the conflict was on. When it was discovered that the Indians were trying to outflank them, Lieutenant Robert Davis took a part of the right line and placed it across the flats to a ridge, thus making it impossible for the enemy to get around the flank, and Captain James Shelby, stationed on a rise, prevented the Indians from surrounding them. The fight now became general, the armies meeting in a hand-to-hand conflict. Both officers and privates fought heroically.

The most interesting scene during the conflict was the fight between Lieutenant Moore and a very large, strong Indian chief. Moore fired at the chief, wounding him in the knee, but not so badly as to prevent his standing, then rushed towards him. The chief threw his tomahawk at Moore, but missed him. Then Moore assaulted him with a large butcher-knife, the blade of which the chief caught with his right hand, and then both men clinched with their left hands. The old savage held the sharp blade of the knife so firmly that his hand was almost severed from his arm, the blood flowing in a stream. Moore, still holding to the handle of his knife with his right hand, managed to get his tomahawk from his belt with his left hand and crush the old chief's skull.

The death of their brave chief caused the Indians to lose spirit and they retreated into the woods, carrying off many of their wounded as they retreated. In this remarkable battle, fought July 20, 1776, none of the white men were killed, and only five were wounded.

This battle was followed by the attack upon Fort Watauga. The fort was defended by about forty men, with Captain James Robertson first in command and Lieutenant John Sevier second. A large number of women and children had fled into the fort for protection. Horses and cattle and such property as could be easily moved were brought under the protection of the guns of the fort.

Old Abraham, a cunning old chief noted more for strategy than for bravery, marched his army along the mountains, through the Nolichucky settlements, hoping to massacre the unprotected people before they learned that he was on the war-path. The people had, however, been warned of his coming in time to get safely into Fort Watauga, but they left their cabins and corn-fields to the mercy of the Indians. The surly old warrior, reaching the Nolichucky settlements, was surprised to find the cabins deserted. Presuming that the settlers had just learned of his approach and were fleeing through the forest to Watauga, he ordered his disappointed warriors to overtake them. Thus in his great anxiety to find the settlers, he left the cabins and corn-fields unmolested. On the next day, after the battle of Island Flats, Old Abraham reached Watauga. He was greatly disappointed when he found out his mistake.

The people in the fort were not so fearful of a sudden attack, as the Indians had been defeated at Island Flats, and at day-break the women were out milking. Suddenly a deafening war-whoop came from the woods. The frightened women saw the Indians coming upon them at full speed, and ran screaming into the fort. One beautiful dark-eyed girl was cut off from the fort by her pursuers; yet, active and swift on foot as a frightened doe, she ran with all her might, her dark-brown hair streaming behind her, evaded her pursuers at every turn, and reached the palisades of the fort. The gates had been closed, but she made a long leap for the top of the palisades. Having heard the screams of the fleeing girl, the gallant Lieutenant Sevier leaped to the top of the wall to help her over. With one hand he shot down the foremost pursuer; with the other, he assisted her in the long leap over the wall. She fell into his arms out of breath and nearly exhausted. This heroine was Catherine Sherrill.

In this memorable siege of July 21, 1776, the savages poured balls and arrows into the fort till about 8 o'clock in the morning without effect. The inmates of the fort returned the fire with such deadly aim that many Indian warriors were killed. A random firing was kept up for some time without effect, but the Indians retreated.

During the attack, a messenger escaped from the fort and hurried off for reinforcements. One hundred Rangers came under the command of Colonel William Russell, but when Russell reached the fort he found that the Indians had retreated.

During this attack at Watauga, James Cooper and a boy, Samuel Moore, went out after some boards to cover a hut. At the mouth of Gap Creek, they were attacked by a band of Indians. Cooper plunged into the river and tried to escape by swimming and diving, but the water became too shallow and the Indians scalped him. The noise of the guns and the screams of young Moore were heard at the fort. Sevier attempted to go to the rescue, but Robertson, believing the firing and screaming to be a feint to draw his men from the fort, prevented him from the attempt. The lad was taken to the Indian towns up in the mountains and burnt at the stake.

Mrs. Bean was also captured by Old Abraham's warriors near Watauga. She had always been so kind and friendly to the Indians that she felt safe on the outside of the fort. She was first carried to Old Abraham's station-camp on the Nolichucky. A white man was also held a prisoner there, and he informed Mrs. Bean that she was to be murdered. At that moment a savage warrior cocked his gun and moved towards her as if he intended to shoot her. Then the chiefs, through her fellow-prisoner, began to ask her how many forts the whites had and how many soldiers were at each, where they were, how much powder they had, and if they could be starved out. She answered their questions in such a manner as to convince them that the white men could not be conquered. Then the chiefs requested the prisoner to tell Mrs. Bean that her life would be spared, but that she would be taken to the Indian towns to teach their women how to make butter and cheese. Later, she was taken to one of their villages on the Tellico and condemned to die. She was, therefore, taken to the top of a burial mound and tied to a stake, around which was piled wood and brush. The flames were about to be kindled when Nancy Ward interceded and commanded the warriors to loose her from the stake. Mrs. Bean's life was spared, and she was finally sent under a safe escort to her husband at Watauga.

The incursions of the Indians continued. The chief Raven marched across the country with the intention of surprising the people of Carter's Valley, but when he got there he found them in the forts. Disheartened by the defeats of Old Abraham and Dragging Canoe, he returned to his villages. A fourth party, divided into small bands, carried the tomahawk and scalping-knife to the people along the Clinch River up as far as the Seven Mile Ford, in Virginia. The Wolf Hills settlement was attacked. The Reverend Charles Cummings and four others were fired upon while on their way to work in a field. At the first discharge of the Indians' guns, William Creswell, who was driving a wagon, was killed, and two other men were wounded. As soon as the firing was heard in the fort, several men ran out to the assistance of Mr. Cummings and his servant, and drove the Indians from their ambush and carried the dead and wounded into the fort.

Two churches had been built in the vicinity of Wolf Hills about 1772, and Mr. Cummings preached regularly to the people. Every man and every boy old enough to bear arms carried his arms to church. On Sunday morning Mr. Cummings, dressed in his neatest clothes, put on his shot-pouch, shouldered his rifle and rode to church. He walked through his congregation with a grave, dignified bearing, placed his weapons within easy reach, and began the solemn services. This pious preacher carried the gospel of "peace on earth, good will towards men," yet he fought as desperately as any other man. Afterwards, as chaplain, he accompanied Sevier in a campaign against the Indians.

England's war-plan had now become well known, and the southern colonies combined against the brutal savages for revenge. Several armies went against the tribes of Indians which had helped in the execution of the plan.

Patrick Henry, Governor of Virginia, ordered Colonel William Christian, of Virginia, to collect the frontier soldiers and march to Tellico and Chilhowee with fire and sword. The gathering was at the Great Island in the Holston, and by the first of August several companies had assembled. This in-gathering of soldiers drove away the Indians from the settlements. Colonel Christian was reinforced by three or four hundred militia from North Carolina under the commands of Colonel Love, Colonel Joseph Williams, and Major Winston. Crossing the Holston at the Great Island, the army marched to Double Springs and waited for reinforcements from Watauga. James Robertson was at the head of the Wataugans, and John Sevier had charge of a select company of scouts. The whole army, including the pack-horse men and the cattle-drivers, was now eighteen hundred strong and well armed. It was made up of infantry, with the exception of one company of light-horse. The old trader Isaac Thomas acted as guide into the Indian country, a distance of about two hundred miles, and Charles Cummings was chaplain.

Sevier was making himself famous in these eventful days. His bravery and presence of mind at Watauga in repelling the attack of Old Abraham and his gallant rescue of Catherine Sherrill, had endeared him to all the community. In this invasion of the Indian country, he gained distinction as a scout and as an expert woodsman.

The Indians had declared that the white soldiers should never cross the French Broad, and they determined to defend it to the last extremity. Being aware of this determination, Colonel Christian sent Sevier with sixteen spies in advance of the main army to the ford to locate the enemy.

Slowly the army moved on through the tangled woods and dense cane-brakes towards the French Broad. Alexander Harlan came by night into Colonel Christian's camp and told him that a band of Indians, three thousand strong, was stationed at the ford, where the war-path crossed the French Broad, ready to dispute the passage. Spies returned and told Colonel Christian that the camps in the bend of the Nolichucky were deserted; but the signs were evidences of the large number of warriors somewhere upon the war-path. The army resumed its march very cautiously and was soon afterwards met by a man bearing a white flag in his gun. His name was Fallen, a trader. The Colonel gave orders that no notice be taken of this man; he soon departed, returning to the Indians and informing them that the pale-faces marching to invade their country were as numerous as the trees of the forests. The army finally reached the French Broad, and Colonel Christian ordered his soldiers to set up their tents and kindle camp-fires, as if he intended to remain there several days.

During the darkness of the following night, Christian ordered a strong detachment from his army to move down the bank to an island and cross the river. The ford was deep, the water sometimes reaching almost to the shoulders, and the current so swift that the soldiers had to wade four abreast to brace each other. Next morning the main army forded, and joined the detachment, the soldiers marching in order for battle, expecting every moment to be attacked. The Indians had a few days before gathered a thousand strong at the ford, and it was from this place that they had sent Fallen to Colonel Christian with a message intended only to deceive. But after Fallen's departure, Starr, another trader, made an earnest talk to the Indians, showing the folly of their attempt to resist the armies of the white men. He told them that the white man was made of white clay and the red man of red clay, and that the Great Spirit had ordained that the white man would conquer the red man. He closed his talk by telling the Indians they had better escape to their mountain villages. This harangue, together with the general feeling of depression over the defeat of Old Abraham and Dragging Canoe, influenced them to return to their mountain fastnesses.

Finding no enemy to fight, the army, having crossed the river, halted to dry their clothes, baggage, and food, for everything, except their guns and powder, was wet. Then the army marched on, meeting very little opposition, and came to Great Island Town, which they took without hearing the twang of a bow. The hungry soldiers feasted upon the abundant supply of corn and potatoes which the Indians had left behind and slept in their wigwams at night. The main army was divided into small divisions, and Tellico, Chilhowee, and many other villages, were reduced to ashes.

But the soldiers came to one village different from the rest. As they entered it, they saw a circular tower about thirty feet in diameter and twenty feet high, covered with dirt. It had but one door, a narrow entrance covered with a curtain made of the skins of animals, and no windows, no chimneys. In it were seats, or places for lounging, made of cane arranged around the wall. This strange village was Echota, the home of Nancy Ward, and the chief village of the Cherokee nation. The round tower was used for a council-house and for celebrating their national ceremonials, such as the Green Corn Dance. None of the soldiers dared or even desired to set fire to this village. By such acts Christian hoped to convince the Indians that he wished to punish only the villages that had been led to mistreat the white men through the influence of the British. In a few days Christian sent some of his men with flags of truce to the hiding-places of the chiefs and warriors, requesting them to come and talk with him, and a few of them came in begging for peace. It was agreed that the Indians assemble the following May at Long Island and make a treaty by the voice of their whole nation. It was further agreed that war should not be waged against the Indians, except those living high up in the mountain towns where young Moore had been burnt at the stake. Against these mountain warriors, Lieutenant Sevier at a later date carried fire and sword with such vengeance that their power was broken.

Christian's army was marched back to Long Island, where most of the troops were disbanded. A new fort, called Fort Henry, was built and garrisoned by a small army, for Dragging Canoe, chief of the Chickamaugas, was still burning for revenge and was likely at any moment to go on the war-path again. Not a man was lost during the three months' campaign. The march, though difficult to make, was one of pleasure to the soldiers, as they were in a strange land, and seeing the strange ways of a strange people. The fertile soil of this well-watered region, enclosed by mountains grand and steep, influenced many of the soldiers to decide, as they trudged along, that they would one day make their homes here. Many of them afterwards moved into this fertile region with their families, and helped to develop the beautiful Valley of East Tennessee as we see it to-day.

These stirring times along the frontiers, and the prospect of conflict with the British east of the Alleghanies, caused Sevier to give up his mercantile business at North Holston Settlement, and offer his services to his country. After Christian's campaign, he removed to Watauga, now the most important of the settlements, and continued fighting Indians in his splendid way—a way which made him famous as one of the greatest of all Indian fighters.

According to promise, Oconostota, with many of his chiefs and warriors, met the settlers at Watauga in the spring of 1777, to make peace. But however desirous of peace himself, he could not induce all the red men to come with him to make the treaty. Dragging Canoe still fostered his passion for revenge, and while Oconostota was at Watauga arranging terms of peace, he thought it a good time to strike a blow at his white brother. He believed that the settlers would not expect an attack at that time, and decided to fall upon them while he had a chance. However, he changed his plan of attack. Reaching the settlements, he divided his men into small parties with orders to fall upon the exposed settlers at midnight. One of his warriors shot and scalped Frederick Calvert, one of the settlers, but Calvert recovered from the wound, only to meet a sadder fate in later years. Old Dragging Canoe himself, with a party of selected warriors, went to Robertson's barn before daybreak and stole ten of his finest horses. Robertson and a few men followed the Indians and surprised them, killing one of the warriors and recapturing all the stolen horses. The old chief, not willing to be outdone by so small a force of the white men, got his braves together and pursued Robertson, overtaking him near his home. They fired a volley and wounded two of the white men, but Robertson escaped with all his men and horses.

This mode of warfare was kept up for a long time, and the settlers formed themselves into vigilance committees to baffle the designs of the savages. Scouts searched the woods day and night for signs of the Indians. One of the most active leaders in the defense of the settlements was John Sevier. He was ever active, ever watchful, always in the saddle dashing through the woods with lightning speed—always to be found wherever the greatest danger threatened. After the treaty at Watauga, Robertson was sent to Echota with the Indians to act as agent for North Carolina, and a greater weight of responsibility fell upon Sevier. His personal magnetism, his cool bravery and presence of mind, and his sound judgment won the confidence and admiration of his neighbors. At the head of his men, he met the Indians almost daily, and left them dead or dying upon the battlefield, without the loss of any of his own men.

The Chickamaugas were perhaps the most formidable of the southern Indians. They dwelt along Chickamauga Creek, near Chattanooga, and on down the banks of the Tennessee, even below the mouth of the Nick-a-jack Cave. This tribe was one of many bloods, being a mixture of the Cherokee, the Creek, and lawless thieves and cut-throats of the white race who had escaped the laws of civilized life and settled in these Indian towns and adopted Indian customs, habits, and language. These Chickamauga warriors had the sagacity of the white race and the cunning bravery of the red race. They had built their towns along the cliffs and in the caves of the mountains along the Tennessee, and felt that the white soldier could never reach them.

Standing on the top of Lookout Mountain, near Chattanooga, the observer gets a view of the country once occupied by the Chickamaugas and beholds one of the most picturesque views in America. The view extends into several different States. The whole expanse, lined with beautiful streams, is now dotted with magnificent towns, making it a historical region sought annually by pleasure-seekers and lovers of the beautiful in nature. The great river cuts through the mountains, making a narrow pass-way appropriately termed the Southern Gate-way of the Alleghanies, and winds its way along the foot of Lookout. Here, looping itself into the shape of a moccasin, it forms Moccasin Bend, then moves along amid the beautiful mountain scenery, past the Nick-a-jack to the Mussel Shoals. Here it loses its calmer motion and dashes into foaming roaring whirlpools too dangerous for the canoe of the red man or the boats of the white man.

Fearing the white men, the Chickamaugas continued to leave their villages and move down the river. They built up Running Water, Nick-a-jack, Long Island Villages, Crow Town, and Lookout, afterwards known as the Five Lower Towns. Realizing the security of these hiding-places of the Chickamaugas and the ease with which they could make a raid upon the white men and then get safely into these fast-nesses, Dragging Canoe continued to stir up his warriors against the white men. If the white men went down the river to settle lands secured by land-warrants, the Indians would attack and murder them. The Nick-a-jack Cave, called by the Indians Tecalla-see, was the greatest retreat and storehouse for the Indians of the Lower Towns.

The Cherokees were held faithful to their treaty by the presence of Robertson at Echota, who always kept his eyes open to all movements of both the British and the Indians; but the Chickamaugas became so troublesome that Colonel Evan Shelby was sent to destroy their towns. In the expedi-tion, Shelby commanded three hundred and fifty men, and Colonel Montgomery, one hundred and fifty. The armies constructed boats, and, guided by Hudson, one of their num-ber who knew well the Indian country, they descended the Holston and the Tennessee to the mouth of Chickamauga Creek. Turning up this stream, they captured an Indian whom they forced to guide them to the Indian towns. They waded through a cane-brake partly sunk under the water and entered Chickamauga Town so suddenly that the Indians, five hundred in number, fled into the mountains for safety without offering any resistance. During this invasion the troops destroyed eleven towns and twenty thousand bushels of corn, drove away large herds of cattle, and seized goods valued at £20,000. These goods had been brought to the towns by British agents, and were to be used to bribe the Indians at a council to be held at the mouth of the Tennessee. The object of this council was to effect a cooperation of the northern and the southern Indians with the British. Thus a second time a simultaneous front and rear attack by the British and Indians was baffled by the hardy backwoodsmen. The expedition quieted Dragging Canoe.

While these events were taking place, Sevier was busy with affairs in the settlements. He sent men and supplies for the relief of Captain Logan, who was besieged at Logan's Station by northern Indians.

A wagon road had recently been opened from Burke County, North Carolina, to the Watauga settlements, and immigration was augmented. The population grew so rapidly that Washington County was divided, a part being cut off and formed into Sullivan County. The opportunities for Sevier gradually increased, and he watched the progress of events so assiduously that he was prepared to act promptly when the time came.

The years of 1778-9 were prolific of notable events in the western settlements. Jonesboro, the oldest town in Tennessee and county seat of Washington County, was laid out, a courthouse and a jail were erected, and the courts of North Carolina were established. Isaac Shelby was appointed colonel of Sullivan County, and John Sevier was soon afterwards appointed to the same position in Washington County.

The establishment of courts was, however, ineffective in checking the depredations of Tories who came to the western settlements. But the frontiersmen arose with the dangers and hardships that surrounded them and dealt promptly with the disturbers of their rights to life and property. They were, as a rule, men of principle and religion; but, when the safety of their country demanded it, they could act with great sternness towards law breakers. Kidnapping the patriotic Whigs was of frequent occurrence. In one instance a party of Tories carried a Watauga Whig to a high bluff up the river and threatened to throw him over if he did not give them all his property. Rather than lose his life he yielded to their demand.

The leader of the kidnappers on this occasion was Captain Grimes who was afterwards captured at King's Mountain and hanged.

Sevier was perhaps the most active and determined leader in putting down these lawless acts. The measures he resorted to were harsh, but necessary; for otherwise the peace and happiness of the settlements would have been destroyed and the plan of the British might have been carried out.

The history of the Watauga settlements reads like fiction. The small number of people in the hands of Providence did wonders for the cause of freedom, and very appropriately have they been called the "Rear-guard of the Revolution."

Sevier had taken a fancy to the Nolichucky Settlement and the fertile land along the Nolichucky River. In 1778 he removed with his family from Watauga and settled upon the south bank of the Nolichucky, at a place called Mount Pleasant. Here, on his rich plantation he began farming with slave labor, though there were not many slaves in the settlements at this time. Again Sevier was in a position to indulge his fondness for horses and dogs. As there was not quite so much disturbance in the settlements, he was at liberty to attend to his plantation with some interest.

But day and night there was a feeling of restlessness thrilling his nerves, for he had still to scout the woods to keep advised of the movements of the Indians. The Indians, always skilled in woodcraft, had learned so perfectly to bleat like the fawn, hoot like the owl, gobble like the turkey, and scream like the wild-cat, that they could deceive the most skillful hunter. Often an unsuspecting settler, hearing, a few yards distant in the woods, the calls and gobbles of turkeys, would take his rifle and creep cautiously through the undergrowth to kill a turkey for food. But soon the noise of his creeping among the leaves and brush was heard and the gobbling ceased; and, as he crept on, the bullet of a rifle would strike him lifeless to the ground. But the white hunters and settlers became even more skillful than the Indians in such games of strategy, and led many an Indian into the snare of death.

Sevier's new home in Mount Pleasant, built of huge, heavy logs, was made large and commodious to accommodate his large family and the friends who chanced to visit him. In spite of the constantly besetting dangers of the frontier life, everything in this log mansion upon the Nolichucky was peaceful and happy till the early days of 1780. Then death came into his home and took away his wife, who had borne him ten children—Joseph, James, John, Valentine, Richard, Betsey, Dolly, Mary Ann, Nancy, and Rebecca.[1]

Sevier's temperament would not allow him to sit down and nurse sorrow, so he kept up his scouting in the woods. The spring months passed, and the summer, and he began to feel sensibly the need of a wife to care for his little ones at home. He fell in love with Catherine Sherrill, whom he had rescued at Watauga four years before. This young woman, whom he playfully called his "Bonny Kate," became his wife on the 14th of August, 1780, the marriage ceremony being performed by Joseph Wilson, a justice of the peace.[2] Her affection for Sevier was shown in her saying, after her rescue at Watauga, that she used to feel ready to have another such race and leap over the pickets to enjoy another such an introduction.[3] "Bonny Kate" bore to Colonel Sevier eight children—Ruth, Catherine, George Washington, Joanna Goade, Samuel, Robert, Polly Preston, and Elizabeth Conway. Sevier was a careful father in bringing up his children, and they made useful citizens.

It was while living on his plantation on the Nolichucky that Sevier's successful scouting and Indian fighting gained for him the nickname of "Nolichucky Jack," or, as abbreviated, "Chucky Jack."

CHAPTER VI

The Voyage of the "Adventure"
and Skirmishes With the British

After the uprising of Dragging Canoe had been quelled, Robertson returned home from Echota. At that time affairs in the western settlements seemed to be improving; families of the best blood from the colonies continued to swell the ranks of the settlers, and the land, rich and very cheap, was eagerly sought by the homeless and poor. The Reverend Doctor Samuel Doak, a graduate of Princeton College, came over the mountain and established in Washington County the first institution of learning in the Mississippi Valley. This was about 1780. He brought his library with him, in sacks thrown across the back of a pack-horse. This apostle of religion and learning taught the sons of the pioneers the more important branches of learning and the principles of religion at a little school building on his own farm. His school was incorporated under the laws of North Carolina as Martin Academy, and later it was chartered as Washington College, and Doctor Doak became its first president.

During the ten years of their existence, the settlements had made some progress in civilization. The habits and customs of the settlers were becoming more polished by the elevating influences of education and religion. The ministers of the

[1] Draper MSS.
[2] Ibid.
[3] Wheeler's "North Carolina," p. 450.

various churches vied with each other in the spread of their doctrines. These educational and religious influences among the strong-minded, brave-hearted pioneers built up the powerful forces which have produced so many great Tennesseans.

Robertson next went into the region of the Cumberland River, where Nashville now stands, exploring in company with several men. During the spring and summer this company planted and raised a crop of corn, and then, leaving three men to keep the buffaloes off the unfenced fields, returned to Watauga for their families.

Sevier and Robertson had been as brothers at Watauga, and it was a sad parting; but Robertson, feeling that Sevier was able to defend the people of the Watauga settlements, determined to go, and set out over-land with several men. Their route was through Cumberland Gap and the southern part of Kentucky. They went slowly with their droves of cattle and loads of goods. The severe winter of 1779-80, ever since known as the "cold winter," made their journey slow and painful. When they reached the Cumberland River, the stream was frozen over so solidly that they drove their cattle over on the ice—an unusual thing in that latitude.

In the meantime, John Donelson, with a few armed men, was to take the women and children and what goods he could in boats from Fort Patrick Henry, down the Holston and Tennessee and up the Ohio and Cumberland to French Lick, where he expected to meet Robertson and his men. He sailed in his own boat, which he called the *Adventure*, accompanied by a fleet of such vessels.

The voyage was begun December 22, 1779. The weather was excessively cold, and hard frosts added to the discomforts of the voyagers. During the voyage there were many accidents and narrow escapes. After sailing for some time the boats came to an Indian village on the south bank. The Indians showed signs of friendship, calling the white men brothers, and inviting them ashore. John Caffrey and Donelson's son got into a canoe and paddled towards the village. They were met by Coody, a half-breed, who advised them to return to their boats. A large number of Indian warriors, with their faces painted red and black, were seen on the other shore embarking in canoes and making warlike demonstrations. Seeing this, Coody urged the white men to move off at once for their safety. He sailed with them a short distance, then, telling them that they had passed all the villages and were out of danger, he returned to his village.

But the boatmen soon came to another village and were again shown signs of friendship and invited ashore. Some of the voyagers, sailing too near the opposite bank in an effort to get out of danger, were attacked by some Indians in ambush, and one man was killed.

Among the voyagers was a man named Stewart, whose family was ill with smallpox. His boat was kept at some distance in the rear of the others, in order to prevent the spread of the disease. The Indians, observing a boat so far separated from the others, fell upon it and murdered the occupants, twenty-eight in all. The cries of the victims were heard by the other voyagers, but they were prevented from going to the rescue.

The Indians continued to march down the river. Finally the boats sailed out of view of the Indians and the vigilant voyagers felt that they were out of danger. But by this time the little fleet had sailed into the Narrows below Chattanooga, and one of the boats was capsized. While trying to rescue the lost goods and restore the boat, the boatmen were fired upon by the Indians who suddenly appeared on the opposite cliff. Everybody retreated hastily to the boats and rowed away as fast as possible. After they had passed out of the reach of danger, they missed the boat containing a man named Jennings and his family, which consisted of his wife and son, a negro man and woman, and a white man. It appeared that in trying to make their escape their boat had run upon a rock and had become partially submerged. What had become of its occupants could not be learned, until one morning, about 4 o'clock, a voice was heard up the river calling, "Help poor Jennings!" It was Jennings himself. After he was landed, he told the story of his narrow escape. He said that the Indians turned their whole fire upon him when they saw he was in distress, and while he returned the fire upon the Indians, he ordered those who were with him to cast the goods overboard and get the boat off the rock. The firing from the Indians became so hot that the son, the young man, and the negro man deserted the boat. Despite the shower of bullets falling around them, Mrs. Jennings and the colored woman succeeded in emptying the boat, and Mrs. Jennings shoved the boat off so suddenly that she came near being left on shore to the mercy of the Indians. The negro man was drowned, and the two young men swam to a canoe and floated down the river. They were met next day by five canoes of Indians, taken prisoners, and carried to Chickamauga, where the young man was burned at the stake, it was afterwards learned. Young Jennings was spared through the intervention of an Indian trader named Rogers who had been released from Indian captivity by Sevier only a short time before.

Again the voyagers moved their boats out into the current. After rowing a few miles, the crowing of cocks was heard in another Indian village. Again they were fired upon by the Indians as they passed, but this time without injury.

The next danger to face was the Mussel Shoals in the southern bend of the Tennessee. The boats were landed at the upper end of the Shoals to see if Robertson had left any sign for them, as he had promised to leave a sign in case it was safe for them to leave their boats and go through by land. Finding no sign, they decided to continue their journey by water. The boats were put in the best possible condition, and the voyage was resumed. The Shoals were very dangerous and their roaring noise added the more dread to the voyagers as they approached them. Gurgling, boiling, dashing into foam and spray, the angry waters roared so loudly that they could be heard for miles away. At times the boats would drag on the rocks, again they would ride the angry waves like ships in a storm. They were three hours in passing over the Shoals and reached the lower end before night.

Below the Shoals the river again widens and the current

is not so swift, and here the men were able to take a much-needed rest after laboring so valiantly at the oars. Floating down the stream quietly for some time, two boats advancing too near the shore were fired upon by a party of Indians, and five of the boatmen were wounded. Reaching the mouth of the creek, the company landed to camp on its banks. After the camp-fires were kindled, the dogs began to bark as if danger were near. Presuming that a band of Indians was coming upon them, the company fled to their boats, leaving behind their cooking utensils. They dropped down the river about a mile and encamped on the opposite shore. Next morning Caffrey and Donelson's son crossed the river in a canoe and returned to the deserted camp-fires to see what had happened. They found the negro left behind the evening before sound asleep by the camp fires. Finding no danger of an attack, the voyagers recrossed the river for their utensils, then sailed to the mouth of the Tennessee without further encounters with the savages.

The voyagers were here made sad by the separation of some of their companions, some to descend the Ohio and the Mississippi to Natchez, others bound for Illinois. The rest of the people had much to cast a gloom over their spirits, for they were without food, worn out by the voyage, and they had yet to stem the Ohio to the Cumberland, then row up that stream to French Lick.

But they never lost courage, and now pushed onward. When they reached the mouth of the Cumberland, it seemed so small that they did not believe it to be the river they were seeking; but, after going a short distance up its current, they were convinced that they were on the right stream. Some of their men had to hunt game for food, and they gathered from the swamps an herb which they called Shawnee salad. At one place some of the hunters found a pair of hand-mill stones set up ready for grinding, but the mill had not been in use for a long time, a fact which convinced them that no Indians were in that region.

The company was rejoiced over meeting with Colonel Richard Henderson several miles below French Lick, for he gave them much information that they were anxious to obtain. Colonel Henderson was surveying the line between Virginia and North Carolina. He informed Donelson that a large quantity of corn had been bought for the Cumberland settlers. The company reached the end of their journey on April 2, 1780, and found Robertson and his men anxiously awaiting their arrival. The tired and hungry voyagers went to their little homes built upon the bluff, where they were rested and refreshed with such food as was common to the pioneer homes.

Thus ended this remarkable voyage. It may be of interest to remark here that the future wife of Andrew Jackson, the daughter of John Donelson, was with her father on this voyage.

Here we leave Captain Robertson, the loved and faithful friend of the Wataugans, to found and develop a new settlement, while his friend Sevier manages the affairs at Watauga and takes an active part in the resistance to British tyranny.

While Robertson was exploring upon the Cumberland, and making the settlements, the thunderbolt of the Revolution fell upon the South. In 1779 the royal army took Savannah and overran Georgia. The Americans, under General Lincoln, assisted by the French fleet under Count D'Estaing, tried to recapture Savannah, but were unsuccessful. Then Sir Henry Clinton sailed from New York and assisted in taking Charleston, the fall of which fixed the fate of South Carolina.

Clinton sent out three expeditions through the country to complete the subjugation of the people. One, under Lieutenant-Colonel Brown, was to occupy Augusta and supply the Indians with guns and ammunition for another uprising; another, under Lieutenant Colonel Cruger, was to subdue the country around Ninety-six; the third and largest force, under Lord Cornwallis, was to move northward, subjugating and plundering the colonies as it proceeded; then, the three armies were to unite their forces to subdue North Carolina and Virginia. Clinton felt that his services were no longer needed in the South, and so, leaving the military affairs in the hands of the above-named officers, he set sail for New York.

The country was full of Tories. These now flocked to the royal standard and swelled the ranks of the British, carrying destruction wherever they went. They left no homes, no food for the widows and orphans. Women, children, and aged men often hid their scanty supply of food in caves.

The whole of South Carolina seemed to be in the hands of the British; but Colonel Charles McDowell, of Quaker Meadows, Burke County, North Carolina, had a very small, but invincible, force of mounted militia at Cherokee Ford, on Broad River. With him was the brave Elijah Clarke, of Georgia, and Colonel James Williams, of South Carolina, each with a small body of brave men ready to die in the defense of their country and of their rights.

On account of the intense summer heat, Cornwallis decided to wait awhile before taking up his northward march, and, in the meantime, he busied himself supplying the Indians west of the mountains with the materials of war, and in enlisting the Tories. He sent Lieutenant-Colonel Patrick Ferguson to the mountain counties to win and enlist the Tories there in his army, for Ferguson was very active and loyal to his majesty's cause. He had winning manners which made him a skillful organizer among the Tories, he was an expert rifleman, and he understood well the arts of war.

McDowell soon discovered the plan of Cornwallis and sent dispatches to Shelby and Sevier for help. The fame of these two men had rapidly spread to the seaboard. As the Wataugans were expecting an invasion from the Indians, who were being armed by the British, Sevier did not deem it prudent to leave Watauga, but he at once collected two hundred mounted riflemen and placed them under the command of Major Charles Robertson and hastened them to South Carolina to McDowell's assistance. A like number under Colonel Isaac Shelby was also sent without delay.

The valiant mountain men added much strength to the little army of McDowell. Together the combined forces now pursued a guerrilla warfare. They were few in numbers at all times, but they were like a mountain torrent dashing down the rugged rapids right into British ranks. Every Wataugan had learned Sevier's mode of warfare, and when the order for battle was given each gave the famous war-whoop and mowed down the enemy with the Deckard. It was the policy of the little army to change camp often and to swoop down upon the enemy like an eagle upon his prey, then dash into the swamps, riding day and night, if necessary, to evade or avoid the pursuing troops of the enemy.

At Thickety Fort, on the Pacolet River in South Carolina, some twenty miles from McDowell's camp at Cherokee Ford, on Broad River, Patrick Moore, a Tory colonel, was organizing and drilling a force of loyalists to be joined to Ferguson's army. Moore's men became so cruel in plundering the helpless that McDowell determined to capture them before they could join Ferguson, and accordingly he sent Shelby with his Wataugans, and Clarke of Georgia with his small force, about six hundred in all, to attack Moore. The little army mounted their horses about dusk and by dawn of next day surrounded the fort. Shelby sent in a demand for surrender, but Moore would not at first yield; he, however, finally surrendered and the garrison was paroled not to serve again during the war. The fort could have been defended easily, but terror seized Moore when such a bold demand from Shelby was made.

Ferguson, hearing of the bold movements of Shelby, determined to catch him and cut his army to pieces. He at once sent a detachment of several hundred soldiers to force him to battle. Shelby and Clarke, learning of his desire, stationed themselves at a point not far from Spartanburg, South Carolina, and prepared for battle. The British advance under Dunlap came up, and a sharp skirmish of about half an hour followed. The Americans fired their loaded pieces; and then, when charged, fought with knives, swords, and the butts of their guns till their faces were so cut and covered with smoke and blood that it was difficult for the men themselves to distinguish each other from the enemy. The battle was hard fought. Sometimes one American engaged two British at once in a hand-to-hand fight. Soon the first advance of the British was put to flight; but, on Ferguson's coming up with his reserves, the Americans retired from the field with twenty prisoners, including two British officers.

McDowell now moved his camp to Smith's Ford on Broad River. As soon as Shelby and Clarke had reached his camp and rested their men a little, they were sent with Colonel Williams of South Carolina, and other reinforcements, among whom was Valentine Sevier, brother of John Sevier, to Musgrove's Mill, on the south side of the Enoree River a distance of forty miles, to rout a large band of Tories stationed there. They took up the line of march before sundown and traveled through the woods till dark, then took a road leaving Ferguson's camp only a short distance to the left and marched all night. Next morning at dawn they met a patrol party, and after a brief skirmish the enemy fled to their camps, which were about half a mile away.

Just then a man who lived in the vicinity approached Shelby's men with an important message. He informed Shelby that the Tories had, the evening before, been reinforced with six hundred regulars under Colonel Ennes. The presence of the riflemen was now known to the enemy, their number small, their men and horses much fatigued with the night's ride, and retreat before a large force of rested men and horses was impossible. Shelby was a man of iron will and quick decision. He decided to meet the enemy in battle. A breast-work was made of logs and brush. In a short time the scouts reported the advance of the enemy. Captain Inman was sent to skirmish with the enemy as soon as they had crossed over the Enoree, and instructed to retreat in the direction of the breast-work. The British came on. Captain Inman's men fired and retreated as ordered. The British rushed after them in disorder, believing that the entire American force was retreating. They galloped at full speed till they were within seventy yards of Shelby's army. Then the war-whoop was sounded, and a shower of lead was poured into the faces of the British. They staggered, but rallied again, and the soldiers on both sides fought like tigers for more than an hour. The Americans yielded at a few points along the breast-works; but they finally wounded the British commander, Colonel Ennes, killed or wounded all his subalterns, and hurled the broken forces into rapid retreat. The gallant Americans pursued them hotly, driving them across the river. In the pursuit of the enemy Captain Inman was killed, and the hard fought battle of Musgrove's Mill was ended.

After the battle, the Americans returned to their horses tethered in the woods, for Shelby was determined to be at Ninety-six before night. Just after the men had mounted their horses, a messenger from McDowell galloped up and presented a letter from Governor Caswell, announcing that the American army under General Gates had been defeated at Camden, and advising McDowell to get out of the enemy's way the best he could. Shelby knew the hand-writing of the Governor, and there could be no question as to the authenticity of the letter. He ordered his men to the mountains, and all day and all night and all the next day they pressed on with as much speed as tired horses can make. For forty-eight hours the men sat in their saddles without a halt till they were far away in the mountains. The men could scarcely be recognized, for their eyes were red and swollen from loss of sleep and exposure to heat and dust. The poor horses had eaten nothing, except what they could nibble from the undergrowth as they hastened along. It was fortunate that they had traveled even so rapidly, for they had been hotly pursued by a strong British force till late in the afternoon of the second day. They now halted for a rest. They were at home in the rugged fastnesses of the great mountains and they did not fear for their safety. They could easily defend themselves in the midst of these bold cliffs.

The little army was now divided. Shelby went back to Watauga; Williams carried the prisoners to a place of safe keeping; and Clarke, with one hundred men, went south, determined, if possible, to wrest Augusta from the hands of the British captors.

CHAPTER VII

The Uprising of the Wataugans

McDowell and his men, chased by Ferguson, later crossed the mountain and took refuge among the Wataugans. Ferguson, giving up the fruitless chase, stationed himself at Gilbert Town, North Carolina, and sent an insolent message to the Wataugans by Samuel Philips, a paroled prisoner, threatening to march his army over the mountains, to burn their cabins, to lay their country waste, and to hang their leaders if they did not cease their opposition to the British. In his army were a few Tories from Watauga who were familiar with the rough passes across the mountains. These men agreed to guide his soldiers to the over-mountain country. Some of them, too, were well acquainted with Colonel Sevier and were eager to betray him into the hands of the enemy.

The message reached Shelby about the last of August, 1780. As soon as he had read it, he mounted his horse and rode to Sevier on the Nolichucky, a distance of fifty or sixty miles. When he dashed up to Sevier's home, his poor horse flecked with foam, to his surprise he found feasting and merry-making going on. Sevier was giving a great barbecue, and a horse-race was to be run. Many people were there enjoying the hospitality of the kind-hearted, great-souled colonel, but the people saw in the stern face of Shelby that some portentous event was impending.

Sevier took no further part in the merrymaking. In two days he and Shelby discussed the state of affairs and carefully laid their plans, for there were many things to think about and many plans to consider. The question was whether or not it would be advisable to fortify themselves at home and wait for Ferguson's visit. To this plan there was objection, as they were also expecting an invasion from the Indians which might take place at the same time they were repelling Ferguson. Besides, this plan was too slow for Sevier. His idea was to pounce upon the enemy, dart swiftly away, and get ready for another sudden attack, just as the smaller birds drive the hawks from their nests. This mode he had often used against the Indians. It was now decided by the two colonels that it would be the best plan, therefore, to collect all the riflemen they could and hasten across the mountains and cripple or overwhelm Ferguson before he could either reach their humble cabins or join the army of Cornwallis. They decided to sound the alarm and call upon the brave pioneers to rendezvous at the Sycamore Shoals on the 25th of September, ready to defend their homes. The two men then separated, Shelby returning to his home to gather his rifle rangers and secure the assistance of the Virginia militia of the upper Holston region, while Sevier was to collect his riflemen and secure the aid of McDowell and his refugees, who were still in the western settlements.

Colonel Shelby sent his brother Moses with a letter to Colonel William Campbell, stating the critical condition and urging him to unite his force with the Wataugans in their efforts to crush Ferguson. To Shelby's disappointment Colonel Campbell did not at first approve of the plan and refused to cooperate with him and Sevier. Shelby at once sent another letter urging more earnestly his assistance. This time the brave old Virginian yielded and brought four hundred of his best riflemen to the rendezvous. Shelby collected two hundred and forty men in Sullivan County, and Sevier the same number in Washington County. To these were added the refugee Whigs of McDowell.

This ingathering of the western settlers for the defense of their country presents an interesting picture. They were a handful of militia, not a thousand strong, unknown to the world, but they were brave and thoroughly determined to fight Ferguson. The men, women, and children of the whole settlement were at the rendezvous at Sycamore Shoals to bid a loving farewell to those they loved, for it was not certain that the soldiers would ever return from the expedition. Provisions for the march had been collected from the little farms. Every boy able to bear a rifle was there, eager to go to war. It was an odd-looking little army. Officers and soldiers were clad only in their hunting-shirts, but they were well armed with tomahawks, butcher-knives, and Deckard rifles. Some of them had never seen war, but many of them had grappled with the Indian warriors, and some had measured swords with the British in Shelby's campaigns, a short time before. Campbell, stern and dignified; Shelby, taciturn and determined; McDowell, easy, dignified and courageous; Sevier, vivacious, energetic and gallant, moved about among their soldiers like gentlemen at a social gathering.

Everybody felt at ease, yet all caught the spirit which thrilled the nerves of the commanders. None feared the British.

It was decided to leave the old men to defend the women and children against any Indian attack that might be made while they were away. The younger fathers and older sons were to go upon the march. One of Sevier's sons was chosen to go with the army, and a younger one, not yet sixteen, wanted to go with his father and brother and begged his mother so earnestly that she called to Sevier, saying, "Here, Mr. Sevier, is another of our boys that wants to go with his father and brother to war; but we have no horse for him, and, poor fellow, it is a great distance to walk." A horse was secured for the little soldier boy, and he went to war and afterwards fought like a little hero.

Old and young came together, eager for war; but who was to defray the expenses of the expedition? Every dollar had been spent in taking up public lands and was then in the hands of the entry-taker. Sevier tried to borrow the money on his own credit, but he could not find a dollar. He went to John Adair, the entry-taker, and told him that the expedition was about to prove a failure for the lack of money to pay the expenses and suggested that the public money be used for that purpose.

"Colonel Sevier," said Mr. Adair, "I have no authority by law to make that disposition of this money. It belongs to the impoverished treasury of North Carolina, and I dare not appropriate a cent of it to any purpose. But if the country is overrun by the British, liberty is gone. Let the money go too. Take it. If the enemy, by its use, is driven from the country, I can trust that country to justify and vindicate my conduct. Take it."

On the morning after the ingathering at Sycamore Shoals, the soldiers arose long before sunrise and began the preparation for the march. While the loving house-wives and daughters prepared breakfast, the men fed their horses. The sound of voices was everywhere heard, the grim war-worn commanders planning the march, the fond wives talking over the affairs of the homes now to be left to their care, the children playing with each other, little thinking of the long absence of their fathers and brothers. The breakfast was served hastily, the horses were saddled, and every soldier made ready for the march. But, before the march was begun, all the armed soldiers assembled and stood with bowed heads while the Reverend Doctor Doak, with uplifted hands, invoked the blessings of Heaven upon them and besought God to fight their battles. The spirit of war thrilled the bosom of every brave soldier leaning in reverence on his long rifle as the grave old minister called on them to be brave in battle and to smite their enemy with the sword of the Lord and of Gideon.

Then the little army took up the line of march. No drum beat the advance, no martial music stirred their brave souls. Only love of home, liberty, and country prompted them to face the dangers and hazards of war. There was no chaplain, no physician, none of the accommodations of modern warfare. "A shot-pouch, a tomahawk, a knife, a knapsack and a blanket, composed the soldier's outfit. At night, the earth afforded him a bed and the heavens a covering; the mountain stream quenched his thirst; while his provision was procured from supplies acquired on the march by his gun."

A few cattle for beef were driven in the rear of the army for a while, but their progress was so slow that they had to be left behind.

The little army, marching up Doe River, soon reached the mountains. Here they encamped. Next morning, traveling up the pass between Roane and Yellow mountains, after hard marching, they reached the top. The bald table-land was covered with snow, and the air was brisk and cool.

At roll-call it was found that two men from Sevier's command, who were undoubtedly Tories, had deserted, and were then, it was thought, hurrying to Ferguson's camp to warn him of the coming danger. The situation was taxing to the genius of the commanders, but they turned quickly to the left of the usual road and went down untrodden passes, than which no more difficult ways were ever followed by an army of horsemen. They descended the mountain into a wild region and crossed the Blue Ridge at Gillespie's Gap. From this place they beheld, in the region of the upper Catawba, the scattered cabins of the settlements which had been made by the Carolinians in the shadows of the mountains. From here they pushed boldly down the river to Quaker Meadows, the home of McDowell. Here they fell in with three hundred and fifty militia under Colonel Cleveland and Colonel Winston. Other recruits eager for war were added to their ranks from day to day.

But they had no chief commander, and the officers met in council to determine who should be their leader. Some feared that the command would fall upon Colonel McDowell, who was too old and inactive for the place. To quiet their fears, Shelby told them that the enemy would likely soon be encountered and that something must at once be done. Accordingly, he suggested that Colonel Campbell be chosen their commander, as he had the largest regiment and was a strong man, every way worthy of the position. Furthermore, it was agreed that Colonel McDowell go in person to General Gates and apply for an officer to be assigned to the command of the little army. No officer from Gates' army ever came, but the riflemen marched on after Ferguson. The several officers met in council each night to decide upon the action for the following day.

The two deserters succeeded in reaching Ferguson's camp, and so, when the riflemen arrived at Gilbert Town, they found that Ferguson had fled. His army at this time was somewhat reduced, a part having been sent towards Augusta in pursuit of Elijah Clark; others being off on furloughs to visit their families. Ferguson was a brave man, but he had a dread of these Watauga soldiers, and could not remain inactive at Gilbert Town and await the return of his men. He broke up camp and retreated through the woods and swamps towards Cornwallis, calling upon the loyalists all along the line of march to hurry to his assistance. But they did not rush rapidly to his standard, for many of them seemed to realize that it was useless. As he hastened along, he sent out a circular letter containing this appeal: "If you wish to live and bear the name of men, grasp your arms in a moment and run into camp. The Backwater men have crossed the mountain; McDowell, Hampton, Shelby, and Cleveland are at their head, so that you know what to depend upon. If you choose to be degraded forever and ever by a set of mongrels, say so at once, and let your women turn their backs upon you, and look out for real men to protect them."

Ferguson sent runners to Lord Cornwallis, informing him of the critical situation and begging him for reinforcements. At the same time he was marching in the direction of Cornwallis.

The riflemen, however, had gained a more exact knowledge of Ferguson's route and moved on in haste to the Cowpens, where they were joined by a few men under Colonel Williams, Major Chronicle, and Colonel Hampbright. The sun had already sunk behind the hills when the soldiers arrived, and being very hungry, they fell to skinning beeves and roasting the flesh on the blazing camp-fires for their supper. Both men and horses feasted upon the sweet juicy ears of a fifty-acre corn-field which belonged to the rich old Tory who owned the Cowpens.

While here the crippled spy, Joseph Kerr, came into camp with tidings that Ferguson was within six miles of King's Mountain. It was deemed proper, however, to obtain more exact information of his position. So, Major Chronicle suggested Enoch Gilmer as the most suitable man in the army, "for" said he, "Gilmer can assume any character that occasion may require; he can cry and laugh in the same breath, and all who saw it would believe he was in earnest; he could act the part of a lunatic so well that no one could discover him; above all, he was a stranger to fear." Gilmer accepted the commission and at once set out on his journey. Within a few miles of the Cowpens, he entered the house of a Tory, and told his host he was a loyalist seeking Ferguson's headquarters. Gilmer drew from the old Tory the exact movements of Ferguson and the communication he was carrying on with Cornwallis. A few hours later, Gilmer was back in camp relating the facts he had gathered.

After supper, a council of officers was held in which it was decided to choose the freshest soldiers, the swiftest horses, and the surest rifles, and fall upon Ferguson before he could flee to Cornwallis or be reinforced. The choice was soon made, and nine hundred and ten expert riflemen mounted the refreshed horses a little after 9 o'clock, and plunged into the wilderness in pursuit of Ferguson. A few eager footmen followed close on the heels of the horsemen and reached the battlefield in time to do their share of the fighting. The other less able men and horses followed more leisurely.

On October 6, Ferguson reached King's Mountain and pitched camp on a rocky, half isolated spur of the main mountain. The summit of the ridge is about five hundred yards in length, from seventy to eighty yards in width, and not more than sixty feet above the surrounding country. Here he felt safe from danger and decided to wait for reinforcements.

After leaving the blazing camp-fires at Cowpens, the backwoodsmen had a hard night, for it was dark and drizzling. It was so dark and foggy that many of the riflemen got scattered in the woods, but fortunately reached their ranks next day. That very night Ferguson and his men lay quietly slumbering in their tents on King's Mountain.

In the morning, just before the break of day, Gilmer was sent to the crossing of Broad River to reconnoiter. As the soldiers approached the river, they heard him singing "Barney Linn," a popular song of that day. They knew now that the way was safe. About sunrise the little army forded Broad River at Cherokee Ford. At the outset they had learned that about six hundred Tories had assembled at Major Gibbs', only four miles to their right, and were arranging to join Ferguson next day. Some of the officers desired to destroy them before finding Ferguson, but to this Shelby and Sevier would not consent. They had conceived the plan for catching Ferguson and they were determined to carry it out.

The clouds turned into a drenching rain; and, during the forenoon of the 7th, the soldiers could keep their guns and powder dry only by wrapping them in their sacks, blankets, and hunting-shirts. The roads became so muddy that some of the horses gave out. But Ferguson's trail became fresher and fresher, and the little army, both horse and foot, pushed eagerly onward in the rain.

At Ferguson's former camping place the soldiers halted in the pouring rain long enough to eat some roasted beef for breakfast; then they pushed forward again. Gilmer had been sent on ahead to secure what information he could. The patriots now came within view of King's Mountain. Halting at a house by the roadside, Campbell learned that Ferguson's camp was only nine miles distant. As he was riding off in full gallop, Campbell heard the voice of a girl calling him.

"How many of you are there?" asked the girl.

"Enough to whip Ferguson if we can find him," answered the Colonel.

Pointing her finger at King's Mountain, she said, with a smile, "He is on that mountain." And he was.

The fresher the scent of the fox, the more eagerly the hounds pursue, so the riflemen pushed onward with greater speed. A few miles farther on, Campbell halted at the house of a Tory. Entering, he found Gilmer dining and hurrahing for King George, while an old woman and her two daughters were waiting upon him. To have some fun, Campbell. in a stern voice, ordered a rope put around the spy's neck and commanded that he be hanged a short distance up the road. The girls wept bitterly and begged earnestly for his life.

After getting out of sight, Gilmer began to laugh heartily and said to Shelby, "Colonel, I found them such loyal friends I couldn't help, from pure sympathy, giving both the girls a smack." Gilmer had obtained all the information about Ferguson's position and forces the officers desired, and a short halt was called to plan the attack.

Some of the riflemen had hunted deer in the region around King's Mountain, and during the previous fall some of them had camped on the spot where Ferguson's army was now perched, hence they were perfectly familiar with the region. From the information they furnished, it was decided to surround the hill and hold the enemy on top and destroy them by pouring into their ranks, from all sides at once, a deadly fire. There could be no danger of shooting each other, as they would all fire up hill and the British would most likely overshoot them.

Before the march was again resumed, a messenger galloped hurriedly up to the army to inform Colonel William Graham that his wife was at the point of death. By Campbell's advice and consent Graham left to attend her bedside.

Orders having been given to march, the soldiers again put spurs to their horses. When within two miles of Ferguson's camp, John Ponder, a man whom Colonel Hampbright well knew to be a Tory, was captured. Searching him, they found a dispatch from Ferguson to Cornwallis explaining his dangerous situation and begging for help. On being questioned about the British commander, the youthful messenger said that Ferguson was dressed in a full uniform, but wore a checkered shirt over it. At this information the Dutch commander, Colonel Hampbright, burst out with a hearty laugh and exclaimed, "Poys, hear dot? Shoot for the man mid the pig shirt!"

Laughing at the Dutchman's words, the jaded soldiers pressed onward with lighter hearts into the very shadow of the mountain. Here they met Henry Watkins, a Whig prisoner just released by Ferguson, from whom they gained exact details of the British fortifications and strength. The soldiers were at once drawn up in two lines to surround the hill, the right line being led by Colonel Campbell, the left by Colonel Cleveland. Then "they moved up a branch and ravine, between the rocky knobs, beyond which the enemy's camp was in full view, one hundred poles in front of them," purposely to cut off Ferguson's retreat if he should attempt retreat.

Chapter VIII

The Battle of King's Mountain

It was now 3 o'clock in the afternoon. The rain had ceased, and the sun had dispelled the rain-clouds and thrown a glorious light upon the battle-hill. The horses were tethered in the woods, just after crossing King's Creek. Every man was ordered to "tie up his overcoat and blanket, throw the priming out of his pan, pick his touch-hole, prime anew, examine his bullets, and see that everything was in readiness for battle." A few men were detailed to take care of the horses; but afterwards, when the battle opened, they hurried up the hill to take part in the struggle, leaving the horses to take care of themselves.

Ferguson had not yet discovered the riflemen. He was perched on the summit of the mountain feeling as secure as an eagle in his eyrie. A sentinel had just returned to his camp and stated that there was no danger at hand. His fighting force numbered a thousand, more or less, and was made up of New Jersey Volunteers, King's Rangers, Queen's Rangers, and many Tories—all well armed and well disciplined in the use of the rifle, the sword, and the bayonet. At the foot of the hill were the backwoodsmen, about nine hundred and fifty strong, clad in their hunting-shirts and skin-caps and armed with Deckards, tomahawks, and long knives. They had had no sleep for many hours and very little rest or refreshment, but every man had energy for a hard battle. The sides of the battle-hill, steep and rugged, were covered with trees and shrubs, making it difficult to climb. On top it was level, but was well fortified with rock-ledges and baggage-wagons.

All things now ready, the regiments of the mountaineers began to move up and around the hill. Orders had been given that when the riflemen were ready to begin the attack they should give the signal by raising the Indian war-whoop. For a few minutes everything was quiet, and the men made haste to encircle the hill. The right column, however, while passing through a gap just below the summit, was discovered by a British sentinel, who gave the alarm. Mounting his horse, Ferguson sounded a silver whistle; drums beat to arms; everything was astir in the British camps; and the soldiers were soon at their respective posts ready for fighting.

Fire was opened on Shelby first. His men begged to return the fire, but the Colonel said, "Press on to your places and your fire will not be lost." Onward they pressed amid the whizzing bullets till they reached their places. Then in thunder-tones Shelby shouted, "Here they are, boys! Shout like hell and fight like devils!" Instantly the war-whoops from every regiment around the hill rent the mountain air; and, before the echo from the distant hills could be heard, the sharp cracks of Shelby's riflemen announced that the battle was on. "These are the same yelling devils," said De Peyster to Ferguson, "that were at Musgrove's Mill."

The British charged down upon Shelby's men, backing them to the foot of the hill; then, reloading their rifles, the riflemen drove the British bayonets back to the top. Campbell, after some little delay caused by crossing a marshy swamp, got up into position on the other side and poured a galling fire into the backs of the British. The Rangers charged desperately, forcing Shelby's men down the hill, but the reloaded Deckards belched fire and lead into Ranger ranks, hurling the men lifeless to the ground or sending them headlong over their breastworks.

The firing now became general around the hill; the whole mountain seemed volcanic. Every time the Americans advanced to the breastworks to pour into British ranks their deadly volleys, the regulars leaped over with fixed bayonets and dashed down the mountain sides with such an avalanche charge that they forced the riflemen to the foot. But every time, in turn, the regulars, scarred and bleeding from wounds, were forced to the summit with their ranks thinned and broken. The rocks and trees which obstructed the bayonet charges furnished splendid protection for the riflemen. The charges were frequent, brave regulars dashing, scrambling, falling headlong over rocks and rubbish in mighty efforts to thrust their bayonets into the bosoms of the riflemen. But these backwoodsmen were fleet and active and generally avoided the bayonets.

The battle's roar reached Colonel Graham who was hurrying to the bedside of his dying wife. He forgot his mission and turned his horse at full speed towards the mountain to take part in the battle, but he did not arrive till the victory was won.

On every side men fought like tigers—fought till their faces were black with smoke and their hair was singed with fire. All around the hill lay the dead and dying. The great-hearted old Dutch commander, Colonel Hampbright, received a ball through his thigh, and the blood filled his boot leg. His men besought him to retire. "No, poys," said he, "I will stay as long as I can sit up." Colonel Williams, pushing into the thickest of the fight, received a wound and was borne unconscious to the rear. Water was sprinkled on his face to revive him. Gasping for breath and looking at his men, he exclaimed, "For God's sake, boys, don't give up the hill!"

Ferguson's men were falling fast, and he darted from place to place. When his men staggered and faltered, he cheered them with the shrill blasts of his silver whistle. The riflemen drew the line of attack near the top. The broken ranks of the regulars charged and recharged, and the conflict was terrible.

Slowly the riflemen forced their way to the summit. Sevier and his invincible Wataugans pressed against the enemy's center and received a bayonet charge from the regulars. The conflict here became so stubborn that the regulars were compelled to concentrate their forces in a mighty effort to cripple or destroy Sevier's division. But the Wataugans did not yield, and were the first to reach the summit and hold their position. Captain Robert Sevier, brother of Colonel Sevier, was mortally wounded in the abdomen and died two or three days later.

As the riflemen closed in their forces on Ferguson's thinned and crippled ranks, the smoke became more stifling, the fighting more stubborn, and the hoarse war-whoops more deafening and frightful. The aim of the backwoodsmen now became so deadly and the British fell so fast that two white flags were hoisted as a token of surrender. But Ferguson dashed up to the flags and cut them down with his sword, swearing that he would never surrender to such banditti.

Captain De Peyster, second in command, seeing the British troops huddled together and shot down like cattle at a slaughter-pen, begged Ferguson to surrender. Realizing that all was lost, Ferguson, with a few chosen companions, made a desperate effort to break through the American lines and escape. He dashed his horse into Sevier's line, cutting and slashing with his sword till it was broken off at the hilt. Gille-land, one of Sevier's men, first detected the man "mid the pig shirt." He quickly aimed at him, but his powder only flashed in the pan. Turning to one of his comrades, Robert Young, he shouted, "There goes Ferguson—shoot him!" Several rifles fired about the same time, and Ferguson, pierced by six or eight balls, tumbled from his saddle and lived only a few minutes. The British broke and ran in among their baggage-wagons for protection against the fatal balls of the riflemen.

The command now fell upon De Peyster, who soon hoisted the white flag for surrender. Following his example, his men raised their handkerchiefs. Most of the firing ceased along the American line, but some of the young men did not understand the meaning of the white flag in battle and kept firing with fatal aim. Others, who did understand the mean-ing, had seen two or three other flags hoisted and cut down, and so they kept firing. One of Sevier's sons, having heard of the fatal wound of his uncle Robert, was so angered that he kept firing into the ranks of the surrendering troops, until he was finally stopped.

De Peyster dismounted and handed his sword to Colonel Campbell. The prisoners laid down their arms and were placed under a double guard. The battle was over. The brave Colonel Williams lived to hear the shouts of victory, then breathed his last with perfect satisfaction. The victory was decisive. Sevier and Shelby with their over-mountain men had come to capture or overwhelm Ferguson; now the brave Highlander lay cold and silent at their feet. The Americans killed or captured the whole of the British force, except a very few who escaped by wearing white paper badges such as some of the Americans used. The whole fight lasted about an hour. The loss of the British in killed and wounded probably amounted to more than three hundred, while that of the Americans was not more than ninety.[1]

Thus ended the battle of King's Mountain, fought October 7, 1780. General Bernard, an aid-de-camp to Napoleon, on examining this battle-ground at a later time, said: "The Americans, by their victory in that engagement, erected a monument to perpetuate the memory of the brave men who had fallen there; and the shape of the hill itself would be an eternal monument of the military genius and skill of Colonel Ferguson, in selecting a position so well adapted for defense; no other plan of assault but that pursued by the mountain men, could have succeeded against him."

The Americans camped the following night on the battle-hill. The next day was Sunday. At early dawn the Americans buried the dead. Ferguson was buried in a shallow ditch near where he fell. Tradition says that his burial robe was nothing more than a beef's hide. The wolves in countless numbers later went among the graves and scratched up some of the dead soldiers. The place, therefore, became a great center for wolf hunting.

Casting lots for Ferguson's personal effects as souvenirs of the battle, Captain Joseph McDowell received his set of china dinner plates and a small coffee cup and saucer; Colonel Shelby got his silver whistle; Colonel Campbell was allotted his papers and correspondence; Colonel Cleveland, who had lost his horse in the battle, was awarded his white horse; and his silken sash and his commission as lieutenant-colonel fell into the hands of Sevier.

After the burial of the dead and attention to the wounded of both armies, the victorious riflemen burnt the British tents and baggage-wagons and began to march in the direction of their homes. The prisoners trudged along on foot, bearing their own arms, care being taken to remove all the flints from the locks. They were at all times kept under a close guard, but they had been so cowed by their defeat that they felt it useless to attempt to escape. The victors pressed on as fast as possible, keeping near the mountains, for they feared an attack from Cornwallis. There was no danger, however, for Cornwallis was then retreating from Charlotte towards the coast. He had received one of the messages from Ferguson and had ordered Tarleton to go to his rescue; but, when he heard of the defeat at King's Mountain and of the exaggerated number of the mountain victors, he quickly recalled Tarleton and sought safety in retreat.

On October 14th a halt was called and a court-martial held at Bickerstaff's Old Field in Rutherford County to try some of the prisoners for desertion and graver crimes. Some of the soldiers and commanders, still remembering the unmerciful treatment which befell the unfortunate Americans while the British were in possession of the South, were burning for revenge. Thirty of the prisoners were brought under the gallows, and the work of execution commenced. After nine of these had been hanged, Sevier and Shelby interfered and saved the lives of the remainder. Among the executed was Captain Grimes from Watauga, who, as we have seen, was the leader of a band of Tory kidnappers in the western settlements.

The army was now broken up. Nolichucky Jack and his braves hurried across the mountains to their homes, for they were expecting an Indian attack upon the Watauga settlements, and Campbell, Shelby, and Cleveland carried the

[1] Schenck's "North Carolina," p. 174.

remaining prisoners to Virginia. Passing through Hillsboro they made an official report of the battle to General Gates, who was there brooding over his own terrible defeat at Camden. The report must have cheered his broken spirit and animated his shattered forces now idle in their tents.

On the arrival of the victorious riflemen at Watauga, there was much rejoicing. We may imagine the solemn mien of Doctor Doak as he greeted them with his benediction, for his earnest prayer had been fully answered in the victory at King's Mountain, which was, in the language of Thomas Jefferson, "the joyful enunciation of that turn in the tide of success, that terminated the Revolutionary War with the seal of our independence."

Chapter IX

Battles with the Indians

Upon his return from King's Mountain, Colonel Sevier was not surprised to hear that the Indians were upon the warpath. He had not reached the settlements an hour too soon. The old Indian trader, Isaac Thomas, and another trader, named Harlan, were there awaiting his return; for they had had a message of warning from Nancy Ward. The country was alarmed, and the people from the remote cabins had left their homes and garnered crops, and fled to the forts for protection. On the march home, Colonel Sevier had sent Captain Russell in advance to hold the Indians in check in case they should attack the settlers before his return. Russell hurried across the mountain and organized the militia to meet the expected invasion.

Without a day's rest, Sevier again sprang into his saddle to lead a campaign against the Indians. He knew they had been armed by British agents, so he proposed to lose no time in discomfiting them. Notwithstanding the fact that he had been in the saddle almost day and night for more than three weeks, riding among the craggy peaks and dismal swamps without substantial food to eat, he started the first week in December, 1780, upon a march with over two hundred expert riflemen, expecting to meet Colonel Arthur Campbell of the Virginia border with his riflemen at the French Broad.

On the second night of the march, he camped at Long Creek, Captain Guess being sent forward with scouts to look for Indians. Ascending a small knoll, the scouts found themselves face to face with a large band of Indians only forty yards distant. They fired upon the savages from their horses and galloped back to camp with the tidings. The Indians returned the fire, but without effect. Sevier prepared to receive a night attack. His soldiers lay on their arms, but were undisturbed. During the night the riflemen were joined by about seventy Wataugans who had come up by forced marching. Next morning the march was resumed, with spies in front, the army pursuing the Indians very cautiously, for fear of an ambush. They found the body of an Indian killed by the scouts the evening before. As it is the custom of the Indians to bear off their dead and wounded, the Wataugans, were, therefore, fully convinced that the Indians had made a rapid retreat, and they pushed on with a more vigorous pursuit. They reached the French Broad; but, not finding Colonel Campbell as expected, crossed the river at Big Island and camped at Boyd's Creek.

Early next morning the advance-guard under Captain Stinson found, about three miles away, the place where the Indians had recently camped. Their camp-fires were still burning. As soon as Colonel Sevier was informed of the fact, he ordered his army to march to the front in three divisions, the center commanded by himself, the right wing by Major Jesse Walton, and the left wing by Major Jonathan Tipton. The scouts were ordered to fire upon the Indians when they discovered them and then retreat towards the main army to draw the enemy into ambush. By and by the soldiers, hearing vigorous firing in the distance, quickly formed in a half moon and concealed themselves in the grass and undergrowth. The stratagem worked well. The Indians followed the scouts furiously right into the center. Sevier's men lay quiet till they were close, then broke their ranks with a destructive fire from the fatal Deckards. Walton's wing fell heavily upon the dusky fellows, but Tipton was too slow, and the panic-stricken warriors fled through the opening thus made to a dense swamp, and escaped. Not one of the soldiers was killed or even wounded but several Indians fell. Many weapons and all of their plunder fell into the hands of the victors. Letters from Sir Henry Clinton and other British officers were found in the captured bundles. This battle has ever since been known as the battle of Boyd's Creek.

After this battle, Colonel Sevier led his men back to the French Broad and awaited the arrival of Colonel Campbell and his men. His prompt action and swift movement had saved the settlements from an invasion. Had he waited for Colonel Campbell, the Indians by this time would have been in the settlements burning, slaying, and scalping.

The Indians now concentrated their forces at the main ford of the Little Tennessee, one mile below Chota, where they expected the combined forces of the enemy would attempt to cross. But the army crossed at the lower ford. Climbing the opposite bank, one of the horsemen saw a large party of Indians stationed on a high place watching their movements. These soon retreated before the riflemen and disappeared from view. The army, after crossing the river, separated into two divisions and burned Chota, Chilhowee, and other towns along the streams. The Indians fled before the cavalry, and the hungry troops feasted upon the corn, beans, pumpkins, and other things which the fleeing Indians had left.

While it was destroying the Indian wigwams, Nancy Ward met the army with a message from Watts and Noonday, who begged for peace. But Campbell and Sevier wished first to reduce to ashes all the Hiawassee villages. On their way to these villages, they frequently skirmished with the Indians, several of whom were killed. In one skirmish Captain Elliot was killed. His body was buried at Tellico beneath a hut, which was burned down over his grave to hide it from the Indians. The Hiawassee villages were burned, the cattle killed, and the grain supplies destroyed.

Although the Indian country had been laid waste, their towns burned, their food supplies destroyed, many of their braves killed, and many of their women and children captured and although the old chiefs, John Watts and Noon Day, had sued for peace, the young warriors showed no disposition to discontinue their warfare. Such stubborn conduct caused Colonel Sevier, Colonel Campbell, and Joseph Martin to send to the chiefs and warriors the following appeal, signed at Kai-a-tee, January 4, 1781:

"Chiefs and warriors, we came into your country to fight your young men. We have killed many of them and destroyed your towns. You know you began the war by listening to the bad councils of the King of England and the falsehoods told you by his agents. We are now satisfied with what is done, as it may convince your nation that we can distress you much at any time, when you are so foolish as to engage in war against us. If you desire peace, as we understand you do, we, out of pity to your women and children, are disposed to treat with you on that subject.

"We, therefore, send you this by one of your young men, who is our prisoner, to tell you, if you are disposed to make peace, six of your head men must come to our agent, Major Martin, at the Great Island, within two moons, so as to give him time to meet them with a flag-guard, on Holston River, at the boundary line. To the wives and children of those men of your nation who protested against the war, if they are willing to take refuge at the Great Island until peace is restored, we will give a supply of provisions to keep them alive. Warriors, listen attentively! If we receive no answer to this message until the time already mentioned expires, we shall then conclude that you intend to continue to be our enemies. We will then be compelled to send another strong force into your country, that will come prepared to remain in it, to take possession of it as a conquered country, without making you any compensation for it."

But the treaty was not made for some time after the "two moons," and the Indians continued to prowl and murder in the settlements.

Sevier felt that the warriors of the towns he had just destroyed would not be so soon on the war-path without the help of some other tribe, and he suspected the Cherokees living high up in the mountains to be the cause of the continued hostilities, and at once resolved to carry the war to their mountain towns. The undertaking was hazardous. The distance was about one hundred and fifty miles, and the trail wound about through the deep, rugged defiles and up the craggy peaks of the highest mountains east of the Mississippi. Sevier selected about one hundred and thirty choice riflemen and began the march. None of the soldiers had ever been in the mountain towns. The faithful old trader, Isaac Thomas, the only man in the settlements who had ever been among the towns of the mountain Indians, acted as guide, but even he had never been over the route they were to travel. He always ascended the mountain from another side. Indeed, it is doubtful if any white man ever tried the region through which their route ran. It was so exceedingly wild and rugged that it had been secure from the invasion of the most adventurous hunter. The mountain streams were apt to be swollen from snow and rain at this season of the year.

Colonel Sevier followed the French Broad, crossed the Ivy and the Swannanoa, two swift streams dashing into the French Broad, and climbed the mountain heights. The trail was at times so steep and rugged that his men had to dismount and help their horses up. By and by the little army reached the neighborhood of the Indians, and the old trader's services were in requisition. He guided the army to Tuckasejah, a village on the headwaters of the Little Tennessee. Sevier fell upon this village with his usual swift dashing charge and soon reduced it to a heap of smoldering embers. He carried fire and sword to their other villages with the same vigorous energy, sparing neither homes nor food, the Indians fleeing panic-stricken. Many of their bravest warriors were slain, and fifty women and children were taken prisoners. His work now done, Sevier resumed the line of march and disappeared in the mountains with his captives as suddenly as he had appeared. Returning by the same route by which they had come, the little army reached their homes after an absence of twenty-nine days, having accomplished the most remarkable campaign in the history of our Indian warfare. Colonel Sevier kept ten of the prisoners for three years and then exchanged them for white prisoners.

Settlers had followed close on the heels of Sevier's campaigns, and this enraged the Indians and caused them very frequently to attack the cabins of the advanced settlers. During the summer of 1781, a party of Cherokees attacked the new settlement on Indian Creek. Colonel Sevier took one hundred riflemen and went down to put an end to the struggle. He struck the trail of the Indians and managed to surround them by his quick movements and, without the loss of a single man, killed seventeen of their braves and drove the remainder into retreat.

Scarcely had the troops reached their homes from the Indian campaign and disbanded, when a messenger came to Sevier's home with a dispatch from General Greene. The dispatch was dated September 16, 1781, and urged Sevier to cross the mountains and help cut off the retreat of Cornwallis, in case he should attempt to make his way back to Charleston. The message had been a long time in reaching its destination, and Sevier lost no time in responding to its call. Collecting two hundred mounted riflemen, he crossed the mountains for another swoop upon the British. Reaching Charlotte, North Carolina, he learned of the surrender of Cornwallis at Yorktown, a surrender which virtually closed the war.

General Greene now suggested that Sevier join General Francis Marion in driving the British general, Stuart, into Charleston. Always eager for action, Sevier and his men sprang into their saddles and were soon with the "Swamp Fox" at Davis's Ferry, on the Santee. The arrival of the overmountain men gave encouragement to General Marion and swelled his little army into a splendid body of cavalry with which he could now inflict a blow upon the enemy.

Stuart was at a place called "Ferguson's Swamp," on the public highway leading to Charleston. Marion crossed over to the south side of the Santee and advanced towards the enemy. Having learned that several hundred Hessian soldiers, stationed at Monk's Corner, about ten miles beyond the camp of Stuart, were in a state of mutiny, he sent a detachment of about five hundred of the best riflemen, among whom were Sevier and Shelby with their best marksmen, under the command of Colonel Mayhem to capture the Hessians.

Leaving the main army of the enemy a short distance to the left, the riflemen in Mayhem's charge pressed rapidly through the woods and swamps, and on the evening of the second day's ride got within about two miles of Monk's Corner. The riflemen threw themselves across the public road and slept on their arms in order to cut off the retreat of the Hessians in case they should attempt in the night to escape to Charleston. Early in the morning, Mayhem sent in a demand for surrender, but the British commander declared that he would defend his post at all hazards, whereupon Shelby decided to take in person the second demand for surrender. So, taking his flag of truce, he advanced to the fort and informed the commander that if he was so mad as to allow his post to be stormed, every one of his men would be put to the sword. He further told him that several hundred of the over-mountain riflemen were at hand and would soon be upon them with tomahawks. The British officer then asked if the riflemen had any artillery? Shelby said, "We have guns that will blow you to atoms in a minute!" In a calmer tone the British officer said, "I suppose I must surrender," and threw open the gate of the fort.

While taking charge of the prisoners at Monk's Corner, the riflemen saw another British post. It was a large brick house, five or six hundred yards east of them, enclosed within a strong abatis, and in it were about one hundred soldiers and fifty dragoons, who could have defended themselves easily. Resorting to strategy, some of the soldiers dismounted and marched in, as infantry, while others, as a body of cavalry, rode boldly up to the house and demanded surrender. The fort was surrendered without the crack of a rifle; and, in addition to the prisoners, three hundred stands of arms fell into the hands of the riflemen. Ninety prisoners were carried behind the horsemen to Marion's camp, but the officers and men who were unable to march so far were paroled.

Stuart tried to recapture the prisoners and advanced to the

outer edge of the swamp which surrounded Marion's camp. Sevier and Shelby were sent out to skirmish with him and lure him into the swamp for a fight, but, hearing that the over-mountain men were in the swamp with Marion, he retreated in disorder nearly to the gates of Charleston.

The British cooped up in Charleston, and civil government once more restored to South Carolina, Sevier and his men set out for their homes west of the Alleghanies, for they knew not at what hour the Indians would again be upon the war-path. When they reached their homes, they found affairs in a ferment. Some Tories from the Carolinas had escaped the vengeance of the Whigs, and were among the Chickamaugas, inciting them to open hostilities. Settlers kept crossing the French Broad and building cabins. The Indians had sent complaints to Governor Martin, and he wrote Sevier about the matter. "Sir," he wrote, "I am distressed with the repeated complaints of the Indians respecting the daily intrusions of our people on their lands beyond the French Broad. I beg you, sir, to prevent the injuries these savages justly complain of, who are constantly imploring the protection of the State, and appealing to its justice in vain."

Another appeal was made to the Governor by the old chief, Tassel. The appeal was as follows, a "talk," full of pathos not common to the Indians:

"Brother, I am now going to speak to you. I hope you will listen to me. A string. I intended to come this fall and see you, but there was such confusion in our country, I thought it best for me to stay at home, and send my talks by our friend Colonel Martin, who promises to deliver them safe to you. We are a poor, distressed people, in great trouble, and we hope our elder brother will take pity on us and do us justice. Your people from Nolichucky are daily pushing us out of our lands. We have no place to hunt on. Your people have built houses within one day's walk of our towns. We don't want to quarrel with our elder brothers; we, therefore, hope our elder brother will not take our lands from us, that the Great Man above gave us. He made you and he made us; we are all his children, and we hope our elder brother will take pity on us, and not take our lands from us because he is stronger than we are. We are the first people that ever lived on this land. It is ours, and why will our elder brother take it from us? It is true, some time past, the people over the great water persuaded some of our young men to do some mischief to our elder brother, which our principal men were sorry for. But you, our elder brothers, came to our towns and took satisfaction, and then sent for us to come and treat with you, which we did. Then our elder brother promised to have the line run between us agreeably to the first treaty, and all that should be found over the line should be moved off. But it is not done yet. We have done nothing to offend our elder brother since the last treaty and why should our elder brother want to quarrel with us? We have sent to the Governor of Virginia on the same subject. We hope that, between you both, you will take pity on your younger brother, and send Colonel Sevier, who is a good man, to have all your people moved off our lands."

Old Tassel did not express the feelings of the Cherokees and Chickamaugas as a whole. At the very moment he was making his piteous appeals to his "elder brother," the Chickamaugas were raiding in the settlements as far up as Virginia. Hence, instead of obeying the Governor's order by pulling down the settlers' cabins, Sevier was again compelled to take up arms against the Indians. He collected one hundred men from his county, and was joined by nearly as many from Sullivan County under Colonel Anderson. All the troops came together at Big Island, on the French Broad. After a few days' marching in the direction of the enemy, they crossed the Tennessee at Citico, where they met a large number of Indians, among whom were Hanging Maw and John Watts. All the chiefs and warriors in council agreed to remain on friendly terms, and John Watts even went with the riflemen to assist in peace negotiations with the whole nation.

After crossing the Hiawassee, the soldiers entered the territory of the hostile Chickamaugas. They soon destroyed the Lookout towns and pushed on to the Coosa River, burning the towns and slaying the warriors. Then, leaving the smoldering embers of the desolated country, the Wataugans set out for their homes. At Chota they held another council with the friendly Indians. After listening to their peace talks and smoking the pipe of peace with the chiefs and warriors, Sevier and his army went quietly to their homes.

For a time the Wataugans engaged in peaceful pursuits. Land offices were opened, and immigrants of wealth and culture crossed the mountains to seek new homes; the forts were deserted, larger and more comfortable houses were built for the settler, gristmills and sawmills were built along the streams, and schools and church buildings were erected wherever the people had need of them. Jonesboro was fast becoming a center of wealth and political influence. A large log court-house twenty-four feet square was built. With the increase of population and the execution of the law, openings were made for the doctor and the lawyer. For a while peace and happiness dwelt in the rustic homes, and the people were free to engage in their sports of horse-racing, and to attend their log-rollings and quilting-bees without fear of danger.

The war of the Revolution had closed with the surrender of the British at Yorktown, followed by the Treaty of Paris, September 3, 1783, whereby England acknowledged the independence of the colonies on the North American continent. There was as yet no "United States," but only a confederation of States of which North Carolina was one, and one having a poorly defined western border.

CHAPTER X

The State of Franklin

In June, 1784, the Legislature of North Carolina passed an act ceding to the Continental Congress all of what is now Tennessee. In other words, the parent State was giving its western lands to pay its share of the recent war debts, which were very heavy. The representatives from the four western counties—Washington, Sullivan, Greene, and Cumberland—were present and voted for the cession. Congress was given two years in which to accept or reject the gift. During this time, however, the jurisdiction of North Carolina was to continue in force.

North Carolina had always neglected her western citizens, and a general feeling now prevailed that they would suffer greater neglect and would be exposed to lawlessness and Indian depredations for two years. No officers had been appointed to call out the militia in time of danger, and the people felt that the time had come for them to act upon their own authority. So they assumed the task of devising a government of their own. Each military company of the three eastern counties elected two delegates to a convention which was to adopt a plan for a new commonwealth. This convention was held at Jonesboro, August 23, 1784. Sevier was chosen president. The delegates were unanimously in favor of a separation from North Carolina, and passed a resolution declaring themselves independent. A large crowd thronged the street in front of the little building in which the convention was sitting, anxiously awaiting the result of the deliberations. As soon as the resolution was passed, it was announced to the crowd and was received with hearty applause. It was further agreed that another convention be held at Jonesboro September 16, for the purpose of forming a constitution and giving a name to the new State. This convention was made up of five men elected from each of the same three counties. For some reason the convention did not meet until November, and by that time two factions had arisen in the ranks of the seceders. One faction wished to act at once; the other was in favor of waiting awhile longer in hopes that matters would right themselves in the end. Sevier belonged to the latter class. In the meantime, having heard of the bold intention of the settlers, the Assembly of North Carolina met at Newbern, October 22, 1784, and repealed the cession act, created the people a new judicial district, appointed an assistant Judge and an Attorney General for the Supreme Court, formed the militia into a brigade, and appointed Colonel Sevier brigadier-general.

Sevier himself felt that there was now no need of going further in the secession movement. On December 14, 1784, when the people were assembled at Jonesboro, he made a short speech on the action taken at Newbern by the Assembly. "Our grievances," said he, "are redressed, and we have nothing more to complain of; my advice is to cease all efforts to separate from North Carolina, but remain firm and faithful to her laws." But the people were more determined on secession than Sevier fancied, and on the very day he made his address, the five delegates from each county met in convention at Jonesboro. Sevier was again chosen to preside over the convention. After he was conducted to the chair, the Reverend Samuel Houston arose and addressed the convention on the object of their meeting, and offered a prayer that they might receive counsel and wisdom from on high in the undertakings in which they were then engaged. A constitution for a new State was submitted and agreed upon, subject to the ratification of a convention to be chosen by the people to meet at Greeneville November 14, 1785. Before adjourning, the convention took action for the immediate election of all the State officials as provided for in the constitution.

Soon after the election, the Legislature met and chose General Sevier Governor. Landon Carter was chosen Speaker of the Senate and Thomas Talbot, Clerk; William Cage was chosen Speaker of the House of Commons and Thomas Chapman, Clerk. David Campbell, who was elected Judge of the Supreme Court, was to be aided in his courts by two assistant judges, Joshua Gist and John Anderson. At this session of the Legislature, four new counties were created, and many acts were passed for the good of the country, among which was one "for the promotion of learning in the County of Washington." In accordance with this last act, Doctor Doak established his school, the first academy founded in the Mississippi Valley. Doak was a graduate of Princeton College, as before stated, and he became a famous teacher. His school building was a plain log house built upon his own farm.

The currency was rudely fixed, the value of the dollar being rated at six shillings. Money was scarce, and a scale of prices was fixed upon almost everything raised or manufactured by the backwoodsmen. The skins of animals constituted the common currency, and were made a legal tender. The salaries of the State officers, taxes, marriage licenses, in fact everything, could be paid in skins or the commodities rated by the Legislature.

Governor Sevier wrote the Governor of North Carolina, informing him in a friendly manner of the action of the western settlers and giving all the reasons for such actions. The Governor of North Carolina replied in a public letter, using his strongest arguments to refute Sevier's vindication of the secession. He firmly declared that the revolting people must return to the parent State, or be brought back by force of arms. He further stated that North Carolina would consent to the forming of a new State at the proper time, but the time, he argued, was not at hand for such an undertaking.

The authorities of the new government next sent a memorial to Congress by the Honorable William Cocke, setting forth the condition of the western people and asking to be received by the Federal Union as a State, but Congress turned a deaf ear to their petition. To make the situation more trying, an unfortunate incident occurred at this time in the Indian country which exposed the people to further Indian depredations and called forth graver censure from North Carolina. An Indian chief, Untoola, was killed by Col. James Hubbard.

The circumstances of the homicide were these: a large inflow of immigrants had consumed nearly all the corn of the settlements, and Colonel Hubbard and a companion had gone to the Indian country to buy corn. Hubbard's parents and brothers and sisters had all been murdered by a band of Shawnees, and he had ever since been an enemy to the Indian race. He had doubtless killed more Cherokees than any other white man. In one of these furious combats, he had unhorsed the chief Untoola, better known among the white men as Butler. Butler had become so disgraced in his nation on account of his defeat that he yearned to kill Hubbard. So, as soon as he learned of the Colonel's visit to his country, he took with him a warrior and galloped off to meet Hubbard in the woods. The warriors met Hubbard and his companion walking and leading their horses. Butler rode up and demanded the object of their visit. "As the war is over," answered Hubbard, "we have brought some clothing which we desire to barter for corn." Then he showed the Indians the contents of one sack and drew out a bottle of whiskey, which he offered them. To convince the Indians of his peaceable intentions, he had leaned his gun against a tree. He then inquired about corn, but Butler gave him no answer. The savage countenance of the old warrior betrayed his wicked intentions. He turned his horse about, as if he intended to make a dash between Hubbard and his gun, or else to get the white men in line so as to kill them both at a single shot. But Hubbard's eagle eyes were fixed upon the maneuvers of the chief; he dared not take up his gun, as that would be regarded as a breach of the peace and renewal of war. However, he reached his hand to the muzzle of his gun, leaving the breech upon the ground, and awaited the attack. Whirling his horse around, Butler aimed a blow at Hubbard with his gun, but missed him. Angered at his failure, the chief then quickly fired at Hubbard, the ball cutting off a thick lock of his hair and stunning him slightly. Both Indians retreated so rapidly that they got eighty yards away before Hubbard could recover himself and fire. But he took sure aim, and at the crack of his rifle, the old chief tumbled to the ground fatally wounded. He begged to be let alone, but allowed Hubbard to lift him up against a tree so he could breathe easier. On being asked if his nation was for peace, the old chief said, "No. They are for war, and if you go any further they will take your hair!" To this Hubbard answered that the Indians would be beaten if they again went to war with the white men. "It is a lie, it is a lie," said the chief. Hubbard then finished him with a blow from his heavy rifle. Meanwhile, Hubbard's companion had his attention so fixed on the combat with the chief that he let the other Indian escape. Hubbard highly censured him for such conduct for he knew the fleeing Indian would soon break the news of Butler's death, and then the Indians would fall heavily upon the settlers for revenge.

On being fully informed of the secession movement at Watauga, the Governor of North Carolina issued a manifesto to the western counties, urging the people to return to the parent State. Governor Sevier issued a counter manifesto to his people, urging them to stand their ground firmly. He endeavored to refute every argument of Governor Martin's manifesto. In November, 1785, the constitutional convention met at Greeneville as ordered to ratify or reject the constitution which had been submitted by Samuel Houston at Jonesboro in November of the previous year. The Commons met in the log court-house; the Senate, in a room of the town tavern. There was bitter rivalry between the parties now headed by Sevier and John Tipton. Tipton's faction was in favor of the constitution submitted by Houston. This constitution called the new State "The Commonwealth of Franklin," and it provided that no person was eligible to office, unless he believed in the Bible, in the Trinity, and in heaven and hell. It further provided that clergymen, doctors, and lawyers should not be allowed to hold office. This strange constitution was rejected, and, on motion of Sevier, a constitution modeled after that of North Carolina was adopted. The new commonwealth was called "The State of Franklin," in honor of Benjamin Franklin, and Greeneville was made the capital.

The affairs of the new State ran well for more than a year, but early in 1786 Tipton and his party boldly espoused the cause of North Carolina. They held elections for representatives and local officers, and reestablished the laws of the mother State. Grave were the conditions that followed. Both parties held courts, and each was in turn broken up by armed men of the other party. Often the men fought each other savagely. On one occasion Sevier and Tipton themselves engaged in a fist fight, but their friends interfered and prevented any serious injuries. Matters grew from bad to worse, and many people were getting tired of such civil strife. The Legislature of North Carolina took advantage of the situation and passed an act declaring that the western counties would at the proper time be erected into an independent State if they would return to their allegiance and wait. A free pardon was offered to all who would return. Many did return, but the majority still stood firm.

The neighboring States watched eagerly the steps taken by the Franks, most of them hoping that their downfall might soon come, as their success might encourage similar revolts in their own western borders. Benjamin Franklin had been informed of the movement, and his advice was asked. He expressed his appreciation of the honor conferred upon him by naming the new State after him, but his advice, like the oracles of the Greeks, was given in vague terms. The old philosopher knew very little of the real story of the western region.

Learning of the wild confusion and the frequent combats between the two factions of Franklin, Evan Shelby attempted to restore quiet. Even his stern efforts brought no change.

He advised that North Carolina raise one thousand militia to force the Franks into submission, but the Governor of North Carolina opposed such a rash plan. Then Sevier persuaded the Governor of Georgia to appeal to the sympathies of the Executive of North Carolina in behalf of the Franks, but these efforts accomplished nothing. The friendly spirit evinced by a manifesto issued by Governor Caswell—successor of Martin—caused the people one by one to return to the citizenship of North Carolina. The Legislature of Franklin met for the last time in September, 1787. Matters had reached such a dangerous condition that the citizens of Franklin could not hold an election. It soon became evident that nothing could be done except by force of arms, and Governor Sevier had not the heart to resort to arms. His term of office expired in March, 1788, and with the expiration of his office the ill-fated State of Franklin collapsed.

The state of affairs was a grievous one to the brave Governor. At first he had advised the people against the establishment of the new State; but, upon finding them determined to revolt, he had cast his lot with them and determined to use his utmost energy for maintaining an independent State. Upon the fall of the little State of Franklin, he doubtless felt that his dearest friends had forsaken him, but they had not. The people probably thought that, as he had advised them not to revolt in the beginning, he would now return to his old allegiance to North Carolina. But they were certainly in error as to their notion of what he would do.

North Carolina, regarding Governor Sevier as guilty of treason, issued a writ against his estate about the time his term of office expired. His slaves on his farm at Nolichucky were seized by the sheriff and carried to Tipton's house on Sinking Creek for safe-keeping. Sevier was at this time on the frontiers of Greene County taking action for the defense of the inhabitants against a threatened invasion of the Indians. Hearing of the act, he at once raised one hundred and fifty men, and with his characteristic promptness marched to Tipton's house to rescue his slaves. It was in the cold winter days of February when he reached Tipton's cluster of log buildings on Sinking Creek. A few days before Tipton had sent a number of his men to capture Sevier, and he had now only time enough to call in about fifteen men to guard his house and defend the slaves.

It was in the afternoon when Sevier halted in a swamp two or three hundred yards from the house. He had brought a small cannon with him and this he planted in front of the house. Having moved his force to this small battery, he sent in a demand for surrender. Doubtless preferring death to an honorable surrender to Sevier, Tipton would not yield, and sent back the reply, "Fire and be damned!" He was so angry he would permit no correspondence with Sevier.

The next day, the weather being rather icy, Tipton's wrath cooled down a little, and he allowed one of his own men, Colonel Love, to carry on a paper war with Sevier. Love addressed his letter to *Colonel* Sevier, carefully ignoring *General* Sevier's official title. In reply, General Sevier stated that *Colonel* Sevier was not in camp, meaning of course his brother Valentine, who bore that title. Night coming on, the correspondence ended. Sevier's men moved back to their camp-fires, and Tipton hurried out messengers for help. Next day some of Sevier's men stationed themselves upon a bluff within shooting distance of the house. During the day a few men joined Tipton. The following night, Robert Love, with a single companion, went to his own neighborhood for help. On the way he met his brother Thomas and about a dozen other men on their way to join Tipton. He warned them of the guard stationed on the bluff near the road. Before it was yet daylight, Love rode his horse ahead of his men, but was not hailed. When he reached the bluff, he found it unguarded. The night was excessively cold, and the guards had gone to warm themselves a few minutes by the camp-fires. Love hurried back to his men with the news and then, raising a whoop which rent the air, they dashed with full speed to Tipton's house. Major Elholm, second in command to General Sevier, proposed the erection of a light movable battery, under cover of which the soldiers could reach the walls of the house. In the meantime, some of the soldiers fired upon the men passing into and out of the house, killing one and wounding another. At last the morning of the 28th of February, 1788, began to dawn. The weather was cold, and the snow fell thick and fast. Several men under the command of a man named Maxwell arrived and marched cautiously within gunshot of Sevier's camp and waited for daylight.

Notwithstanding the fast falling snow and the cold gales which swept from the north, Sevier's men, at the break of day, filed out to attack Tipton's men. Maxwell's troops fired a volley and raised a deafening shout. The men in the house, knowing that deliverance was at hand, sent up another shout which filled Sevier's shivering, half-clad troops with terror, and caused them to flee pell-mell into the woods. The sheriff of Washington County was mortally wounded. The cannon of Sevier's battery fell into the hands of Tipton, and many of the Franks were taken prisoners, among them two of Sevier's sons, James and John. Tipton declared that he would hang them both. Learning of Tipton's threat, the two boys sent for Mr. Thomas and others with whom they were on good terms, and asked them to appease the wrath of Tipton and save their lives. These men went at once to Tipton and pleaded their cause well. They pictured to him the wretchedness of his own sons, whom he supposed to be in the hands of Sevier and about to be hanged for deeds imputed to himself, their father. With tears streaming down his cheeks, Tipton declared that he was too womanish for any manly office, and refrained from carrying out his threat.

Maxwell's men did not pursue Sevier's men more than two hundred yards. It was indeed a curious kind of warfare, not often met with in history, and seems ludicrous though it is significant of the conditions in those frontier settlements. The casualties were probably the result of accident. It was a sham battle in which Sevier tried to regain his slaves from Tipton. Although shamefully mistreated and insulted by the acts of Tipton, Sevier did not go there to shed blood. He could easily have taken Tipton on the day of his arrival, and his little battery could have blown the houses to pieces. "We did not go there to fight," said Doctor Taylor, who was there during the siege, "neither party intended to do that. Many on both sides were unarmed, and some who had guns did not even load them. Most of us went to prevent mischief, and did not intend to let the neighbors kill one another. Our men shot into the air, and Sevier's men into the corner of the house. As to the storms of snow keeping the men from taking sure aim, it is all a mistake. Both sides had the best marksmen in the world, men who had often killed a deer, and shot it in the head, too, when a heavier snow was falling. The men did not try to hit anybody. They could easily have done so if they had been enemies."

Forebodings of this curious battle might have been read in the face of John Sevier as he had sat the previous night in grim silence by his camp-fire. He had often drawn his sword for his country and triumphed over his enemy, but to draw his sword against his fellow-citizens was more than he had a heart to do. "The men under his command," says Doctor Ramsey, "exhibited the same altered behavior. In all their campaigns, order and enthusiasm attended the march, care and vigilance the bivouac, the mirthful song and the merry jests were heard in every tent. On these occasions it was the custom of Sevier to visit every mess and to participate in their hilarity. He spoke of the enemies and danger before, and friends and homes behind them. He was the companion and friend and idol of his soldiery. But now the camp of the Governor of Franklin was dreary and cheerless. No merry laugh was heard—nor song—nor jest. Little care and less vigilance was taken in placing out the sentinels. Sevier was silent, appeared abstracted, thoughtful, and, at this time only in his whole public life, morose and ascetic. Elholm's vivacity failed to arouse him. He communicated little to that officer; he said nothing to his men. He took no precaution, suggested no plan, either of attack or defense."

Had Tipton had the feeling of brotherly love which throbbed in the sympathetic heart of John Sevier, they could have met without the flag of truce and grasped each other's hands in mutual friendship, forgetting all the struggles of the little State of Franklin. Tipton was at first a strong advocate of the Franklin movement, but, when he found that Sevier was determined to cast his life and fortune with the lot of his friends and comrades, he espoused the cause of North Carolina, and did all in his power to undermine Sevier and cause his downfall, for he knew that Sevier was the idol of the people.

CHAPTER XI

Unhappy Events on the Western Border

Slowly, listlessly, and sadly, Sevier and his men wended their way toward their homes as if they were in a funeral procession. He doubtless felt that as many of his best friends had turned their backs upon the State of Franklin, they had also lost their friendship for him as well. In this, however, he was mistaken, as we shall see. And then, too, he was returning home without his slaves, which circumstance bore heavily upon his melancholy feelings. But while he trudged along, nursing his grief, messengers from the border settlements rode up and apprised him of a recent uprising of the Indians, and urged him to hurry to the defense of the settlers. The weight of despondency at once fell from him. "In a moment," says Doctor Ramsey, "Sevier was himself again, elastic, brave, energetic, daring, and patriotic. At the head of a body of mounted riflemen he was at once upon the frontier to guard and protect its most defenceless points."

While Sevier was on the border defending the settlers, his enemies were accusing him of deeds which he never committed, of crimes of which he never dreamed, of intentions which never entered his mind. These misrepresentations, so numerous and base, were not long in reaching Governor Johnson of North Carolina. He wrote to General Martin, an enemy of Sevier's in the western settlements, these words: "Sevier, from the state of his conduct set forth in your letter, appears to be incorrigible, and I fear we shall have no peace in your quarter till he is proceeded against to the last extremity." Governor Johnson was a good man and supposed the news he was receiving to be true.

But however he might be slandered, Sevier was still popular among the western settlers and their chief dependence in the hour of danger. We see him now on the frontier calling out the bordermen and leading them to battle as one having authority. From Major Houston's Station, he and James Hubbard issued this address "to the inhabitants in general," on July 8th, 1788:

"Yesterday we crossed Tennessee with a small party of men, and destroyed a town called Toquo. On our return we discovered large trails of Indians making their way towards the place. We are of the opinion their numbers could not be less than five hundred. We beg leave to recommend that every station be on their guard; that also, every good man that can be spared will voluntarily turn out and repair to this place, with the utmost expedition, in order to tarry for a few days in the neighborhood and repel the enemy, if possible. We intend waiting at this place some days with the few men now with us, as we can not reconcile it to our own feelings to leave a people who appear to be in such great distress."

In the month of May the Indians massacred John Kirk's family, which lived on the southwest side of Little River, twelve miles south of Knoxville. Mr. Kirk was absent from his home, and an Indian by the name of Slim Tom, well known to the family, came into the cabin and asked for food. Mrs. Kirk thought the Indian was still friendly and gave him the food and he departed. But he had come as a spy. After a short time he returned with a band of Indians who had been hiding in the woods and massacred the whole family, eleven in all, leaving their mangled bodies in the yard. When Mr. Kirk and his eldest son returned, they at once sounded the alarm in the neighborhood and the bordermen gathered quickly to punish the Indians. At this time Joseph Martin was living among the Cherokees. He did not believe the Cherokees were responsible for all the crimes committed against the white men in the lower settlements. The Creeks and the

Chickamaugas were generally the ones that stirred up the strife; but the white men suspected, of course, that the Cherokees were the guilty ones, as they lived closest to the settlements. A council was held, and the Cherokees stated that the Creeks kept passing through their country to war on the white men and swore that they were not guilty of the crimes of which they had been accused.

The outrages continued. While passing down the Tennessee, a large boat containing forty white men was captured by the Chickamaugas, and all but three of the white men were murdered. Martin left Chota on the 24th of May and went to the French Broad to prevent mischief. There he found the militia gathered, with Sevier at their head, ready to invade the Indian country. Seeing this martial array, Martin deemed it useless to attempt further to prevent war. So he hurried back to Chota to look after his slaves and other property. Then Sevier made a dash through the Indian country with a hundred mounted men, destroyed a town on the Hiawassee, and killed many of the Indians. His swift dashes carried the same work of destruction to a few other towns.

But on one occasion the record of his brave riflemen was stained with crime. Abraham, a friendly Indian, and his son, remained in their cabin on the north bank of the Tennessee and openly declared that they would not go to war against the white men. When the troops came to the south bank, Hubbard sent for Abraham to come over the river to the troops. After he had crossed over, Hubbard sent him back after Corn Tassel, and others, stating that the white men wished to talk with them. Flags were held out to lure the Indians across. But, as soon as the Indians were crossed over, they were thrust into a house; and, during Sevier's absence, young Kirk, son of John Kirk, whose family had been murdered by Slim Tom, entered the cabin and slew all the Indians with his tomahawk. When Sevier returned, he was enraged at this breach of faith and rebuked young Kirk severely. Kirk retorted that Sevier himself would have done the same if his family had been murdered by the Indians. With no power as an officer, except to lead to battle, Sevier was unable to punish the boy. Most of the better class of the bordermen disapproved of this deed of Kirk, and some went so far as to forsake Sevier temporarily. The terror arising from Chucky Jack's raids and the news of the murder of the chiefs on the Tennessee, created such a panic among the Indians that many of them fled across the mountains to North Carolina for food and protection. Some also joined the Chickamaugas. As soon as a much exaggerated report of the raid reached the Governor of North Carolina, he ordered Judge Campbell to issue a warrant for the arrest of Sevier, but, being a true friend of Sevier's, Campbell refused to issue the warrant.

The Indians, especially the Chickamaugas and a few Cherokees, became desperately furious in their rage after the murder of their chiefs, and fell upon the frontier cabins. The people ran into the forts and relied upon Sevier to protect their lives and their homes. Martin had succeeded Shelby as commander of the militia and was the officer directed by North Carolina to put down the Indian uprisings. But he was better with the use of his tongue than with his sword, and tried to keep the Indians quiet by talks. However, on one occasion, he led a body of militia into the Chickamauga country, near Chattanooga, burning a town or two, but he was worsted in a fight on Lookout Mountain. When he departed from the region, he was followed and harassed for a great distance by the bold Chickamaugas. Sevier was the only leader in the Southwest who could successfully wage war against these brutal savages. The other officers were slow and depended too much upon large forces. The Indians could commit their murders and be in their hiding places before their cumbrous armies could strike a blow. With a hundred or two of his riflemen, Sevier could dash through the forests with lightning speed and strike the savages with such force that they would flee in wild confusion in every direction.

After quelling the Indians, Sevier decided to return to his home. He had a true forgiving spirit and surely fancied he would be forgiven by a people he had so often saved from ruin. But it was not so. Judge Spencer, one of North Carolina's principal judges, who had recently held court at Jonesboro, had already ordered his arrest for high treason. Sevier appeared freely in all public places. With a few friends he entered Jonesboro. Here he found that Martin had been holding a council with his militia officers, and that Tipton was there. The council was just breaking up as Sevier arrived. During the day he had an altercation with one Caldwell. After leaving the town, Sevier was followed by Caldwell, Tipton, and eight or ten others of like character. They went to the house where Colonel Love lodged and got him to go with them to Colonel Robertson's. Here Tipton had a close search made, as he expected to find Sevier concealed somewhere about the place. The night was far spent; and, failing to find the object of their search, they hurriedly set out to Widow Brown's home, reaching her house about sunrise. Mrs. Brown had just risen when Tipton and his men galloped up to her door. She knew Tipton well and doubtless anticipated the object of his visit, for she sat down in the door-way to prevent his entering the house. The bustle between her and Tipton awoke Sevier, who slept near one end of the house. He sprang from his bed and looked through a key-hole in the door to see what the trouble was about. At a glance he understood it all. Seeing Colonel Love, he opened the door and held out his hand, saying, "I surrender to you," and Colonel Love led him to the place where Tipton was contending with Mrs. Brown for entrance into her house.

On seeing Sevier, Tipton swore that he would hang him. Sevier was really afraid that he would be shot on the spot by the maddened demagogue who held a pistol in his hand. But he finally calmed down and ordered Sevier to get his horse, for he was eager to be off with his prisoner to Jonesboro. At Sevier's request Colonel Love accompanied him to Jonesboro. On the way he requested the Colonel to use his influence to have him imprisoned at Jonesboro, instead of being sent so far across the mountains. Love did not approve of this. "Tipton," said he, "will place a strong guard around you there; your friends will attempt a rescue, and bloodshed will be the result." Sevier assured Love that he would dissuade his friends from rash measures. It was a bitter trial to Sevier to be taken from his family and friends, without a just cause; but, under the circumstances, it was impossible to prevail upon his captors to yield to his request.

When they reached Jonesboro, Tipton ordered hand-cuffs to be put on Sevier. This being done, he went a short distance with his prisoner and then left him in the custody of the deputy sheriff and two other men, George French and Gorley, with orders to carry him to Morganton or lower down, if necessary, and put him in jail.

Colonel Love traveled with Sevier till late in the afternoon, then returned home. Before his departure, Sevier requested him to send word of his capture and imprisonment to "Bonny Kate," and to tell her to send him some money and clothes. There is a tradition that George French had orders from Tipton to kill Sevier and that, while on Iron Mountain, on their way to North Carolina, Gorley revealed the plot. On learning the intentions of his captors, Sevier attempted to escape, but during the flight his horse got entangled in some trees and brush thrown down by a recent storm and could get no farther. French pursued and fired his pistol in Sevier's face, doing no harm, however, except to burn his face with the powder. It appears that the ball had dropped out of the pistol in the pursuit.

The officers moved down the mountain and in due time reached Morganton, where they delivered their prisoner to William Morrison, the sheriff of Burke County. Here Sevier was met by two of his old friends, Generals Charles and Joseph McDowell, who became his bondsmen for his appearance at court, and he visited his brother-in-law, several miles from town. He made his visit and returned to the sheriff at Morganton on the second day after leaving. Sheriff Morrison had had the good fortune to share in the honors of King's Mountain, and of course was as lenient towards Sevier as he could be, consistent with his duty.

The news of the capture and supposed imprisonment of Sevier had by this time spread among the western settlements, and the people there were excited and angry. They were fully determined to rescue him. They could see the State of Franklin fall, but they could not stand in silence and see such men as Tipton take their friend and imprison him on false charges.

The story of the rescue of Sevier has been told in different ways, colored more or less by tradition. One of them runs that he was rescued during his trial in court by his friends and sons who had brought his favorite racehorse. When he understood the plot, he escaped from court, mounted his horse, and was soon out of reach of danger. This tale, however, is only romance, for there was no court in Morganton at this time. Sevier's son John was with the crowd that went to Morganton to secure his father's release, and has left a statement of the circumstances under which he made his escape, which is here printed for the first time:

"Immediately after the fall campaign of 1788, Colonel Sevier was arrested and taken to North Carolina. Gourley and French guarded him, and French shot at him. When they delivered their prisoner to the jailer at Morganton, who had fought at King's Mountain, he knocked off the irons from his hands and told him to go where he pleased, not, however, to leave the place. Joseph Sevier, the Colonel's brother, John Sevier, Jr., (the informant), George North, Doctor James Cozby, Jesse Green, and William Matlock went after the Colonel; when within a few miles of Morganton, they stopped one night with Uriah Sherrill, brother-in-law to Colonel Sevier, from whom they learned that the Colonel was not confined and was treated with great lenity. Next morning they rode into town all together, no court sitting, the sheriff absent, went to a tavern, there found Colonel Sevier in company with Major Joseph McDowell; told him frankly they had come for him and that he must go. After tarrying an hour or two, without any fear from the jailer or any one else, Colonel Sevier ordered his horse and all started off before noon, in the most open and public manner, and returned home. They did not know but the sheriff might possibly follow them, when he heard of Colonel Sevier's return home, but he did not."[1]

The backwoodsmen were much rejoiced over Sevier's return, and Tipton, aware of the hostile feeling along the frontier over his act, never again attempted to have him put in irons.

It may be remarked here that Andrew Jackson,[2] then a young lawyer about twenty-one years old, who had crossed the mountains riding his race-horse, a pair of holsters buckled across the front of his saddle, leading another horse on whose back was a shot-gun and a well filled pair of saddle-bags, and followed by a large pack of hounds, was at Jonesboro, just beginning his career. If he took any part either for or against Sevier, no mention is made of it in any of the records.

Sevier was still technically an outlaw but he was held in the highest esteem by all his neighbors, and, at the very first election, he was chosen to represent his district in the State Senate of North Carolina. No man dared to arrest him again for high treason, because all feared the vengeance of the backwoodsmen. In November, 1789, he went to Fayetteville, then the State capital, to take his seat. At first he was not allowed to take it, because the act offering pardon and oblivion to the Franks who returned as citizens of North Carolina expressly stated that it "should not entitle John Sevier to the enjoyment of any office of profit, of honor or trust, in the State of North Carolina." When Mr. Amy, from Hawkins County, introduced a resolution to withdraw the charges against Sevier, and to restore him to the full rights of citizenship, Tipton, who was also a member of the Legislature, opposed it so strongly that a personal encounter with Mr. Amy would have resulted had it not been for the intervention of friends.

Colonel Roddy, from Greene County, censured Mr. Amy for using words so sarcastic as to offend Mr. Tipton, stating that he should be cautious to use such language as would "soothe his feelings." It was suggested, and finally agreed, that Colonel Roddy continue the discussion the next day. But, as the story goes, the Colonel had not been upon the floor long till he had infuriated Tipton, who instantly sprang from his seat and seized him by the throat. Being amused at the turn of affairs, Amy chuckled out, "Soothe him, Colonel—soothe him!" We can only suppose that the Colonel did soothe him, for the resolution was passed and Mr. Sevier took his seat in the Senate of North Carolina. From this time on, Tipton's name seems to become less and less important, but that of "Nolichucky Jack" rises higher and higher.

As soon as North Carolina ratified the Federal Constitution, in 1789, Sevier was elected to the Federal Congress without opposition and took his seat in the following June, as the first representative in the National Congress from the Mississippi Valley. While in Congress he was a modest but faithful member and served the best interests of his people and his country in whatever capacities he chanced to be placed.

[1] Draper MSS.
[2] Allison's "Dropped Stitches in Tennessee History."

CHAPTER XII

The Territory South of the Ohio River

The citizens of the State of Franklin were in no better condition when they came out of the trouble occasioned by their secession from North Carolina than when they went into it. The people living south of the French Broad and the Holston were left exposed to the Indians. During the existence of the State of Franklin, they had lived in an organized county, but now North Carolina refused to recognize them, claiming that they were intruders upon Indian lands. They were troubled, furthermore, by lawless men who were lurking about in the settlements and committing frequent outrages. Fortunately the Indians were at peace in their wigwams since Nolichucky Jack had humbled their passion for war. The exposed and neglected people appealed to General Sevier for help, which he promptly and cheerfully gave. By his help they were organized into an association for protection, and order was restored. The people in this little republic, which we will designate as the Settlement South of the Holston and the French Broad, signed the Articles of Association under which they continued to live till February 25th, 1790, when North Carolina again ceded to Congress all her territory west of the Alleghanies. The gift was accepted this time on April 2, and, by August 7, the land ceded was formed, with all other lands south of the Ohio River, into the "Territory Southwest of the River Ohio."

President Washington nominated Honorable William

Blount as Governor of the Territory, and the choice was a wise one. Mr. Blount was a gentleman of Cavalier ancestry, descended from a Royalist baronet, a man of handsome presence, manly bearing, courtly manners, eloquent address,— indeed, a man of rich culture and commanding influence. He was well known to Washington and was doubtless appointed to the new position on account of their friendly relations. As soon as Governor Blount arrived to fill his new position, he made his residence at the home of William Cobb, a wealthy farmer who had emigrated from North Carolina. Mr. Cobb's backwoods mansion was plain, but well supplied with such furnishings as were common to the wealthy pioneer homes. He kept his horses, dogs, and rifles available for the use of his visitors. He was himself rather courtly, in his rough way, and his entertainment was just such as suited the taste of Governor Blount.

David Campbell and Joseph Anderson were appointed judges for the Territory. Washington gave to John Sevier and James Robertson each the rank of brigadier-general. Sevier was to command the militia of Washington District, and Robertson, that of Miro District. All the powers of government were thus held and administered by five officers, but provision was made for a Legislative Council and a House of Representatives when the number of adult free men should reach five thousand. Provision had also been made to admit the Territory into the Union as a State when the census showed a total population of sixty thousand white inhabitants.

Governor Blount entered at once upon the active discharge of his duties. After appointing the officers for Washington District, he went to the Cumberland Settlement and appointed the officers for Miro District. Everywhere he won the esteem and confidence of the people by his honesty of purpose and courteous manners.

At New York, Washington had made a treaty with the Creek Nation, the famous chief, McGillivray, being the most prominent Indian present. In order to dispel the clouds of war which continually hung over the settlers south of the Holston and the French Broad, it was necessary to obtain from the Indians all the lands upon which the white men had settled. Governor Blount sent a messenger to Echota inviting the Cherokees to a council to be held in the month of May at White's Fort on the Holston River.

White's Fort was on the spot where the beautiful city of Knoxville now stands. The place was first visited in the summer of 1787 by two soldiers of the Revolution, James Connor and James White, from Iredell County, North Carolina. These old soldiers held land warrants as pay for their services in the Revolution and were exploring to find a place suitable for their future homes. The fertile soil, the noble hills, the good supply of water, the stately trees of the ancient forest, at once led these old heroes to build White's Fort, clear the forest for cornfields, and return for their families and friends. This furnished the nucleus of an important settlement which grew, in time, to be a handsome city. When the month of May came, the Indians failed to meet Governor Blount in council. Some men had spread the rumor among them that the Governor intended to draw them into a treaty and award them the same fate that had befallen Old Tassel. To convince the Indians of the falsity of this rumor, Robertson rode from Nashville to Echota to talk with them. They still had the utmost confidence in Robertson and, after hearing his talk, decided to attend the council at a later date.

It was, consequently, late in June when the Cherokees assembled at White's Fort for the council. The weather was fair, and fully twelve hundred Indians came with the chiefs. Even several squaws, with their papooses, were there. The treaty-ground was at the foot of what is now Water Street, Knoxville, under the tall trees shading the banks of the Holston. Here, tradition tells us, the Governor, in full military dress, with his three-cornered hat and gold-mounted sword, met the Indians and was introduced to the chiefs. Many white people were gathered in groups on the ground to behold the council. None came armed. The white men gave way to the custom of the Indian council house. The Indians sat upon the ground in a circle around the speaker, listening in silence with fixed attention to what was said. The warriors were decorated with eagles' feathers. Governor Blount sat near his tent, and his civil and military officers stood near him with their hats off in token of respect to the Governor and the chiefs and warriors. In the midst of the officials stood a gallant hero whom every Indian there loved and feared. This hero was the famous Nolichucky Jack. They gazed with interest upon this man, who had so often scattered their savage forces to the winds by his lightning dashes, and they must have been surprised to see so great a soldier now with such a quiet, modest bearing.

On July 2nd a treaty was signed and the pipe of peace was smoked. By this treaty the white people got from the Indians the lands upon which the settlements had been made. The white men then returned to their plantations to engage in the various pursuits of farm life; the Indians, to their wigwams to brood over what had been done. In this treaty the Indians acknowledged themselves under the sole protection of the United States and agreed to a perpetual friendship with its citizens. All prisoners were to be exchanged. The citizens of the United States were to have free navigation of the Tennessee River and the undisturbed use of a road from Washington County to Miro District. For the lands secured, the Indians were given presents and valuable goods and an annuity of one thousand dollars. Afterwards five hundred dollars more were added to the annuity.

Soon after the treaty, White's Fort settlement grew larger. Many of the people who had attended the treaty were impressed with the fertile soil and the favorable location of the growing settlement, and moved their families there. The population increased so rapidly that a large settlement was formed along the banks of the Holston, and Governor Blount established the capital of the Territory there. James White, the venerable proprietor, laid out a town and called it Knoxville in honor of General Knox, who was then Secretary of War. A court-house and a jail were built of heavy hewn logs.

Negotiation with Spain for the free navigation of the Mississippi was still pending, and the United States desired to maintain friendly relations with the Spaniards, who had worked themselves into the good graces of most of the Creeks and Cherokees. The Spaniards traded with the Indians freely and told them that the king of Spain would protect them against the encroachments of the Americans on their hunting-grounds. They thus made a cat's paw of the Indians, working out their own selfish policy in trying to force the western people to secede from the United States, in order that they might get for Spain all the rich land within the present limits of Tennessee. The officers of the Territory treated the Spaniards with courtesy, and were commanded to act only on the defensive against the Indians. This policy seemed good and wise, as one rash act might cause the balance of friendship to tremble. But the Spanish traders and agents in the Indian towns soon caused the faithless warriors to forget the pledges made at White's Fort. Hostilities broke out on the frontiers, and the settlers were again threatened with depredations from the Indians. Sevier could not use his former tactics against the foe, for he had to act strictly on the defensive. He built a chain of blockhouses along the frontier and moved his family to his own station, which was about five miles south of Knoxville. His log residence was large and comfortable and strongly built to resist the attacks of the Indians. For nearly three years of Blount's administration Sevier was kept busy ranging the woods in search of the Indian depredators or marching into their country burning their villages and destroying their crops. He did not adhere solely to defensive tactics; indeed he could not, as we shall soon discover.

After Sevier had moved to his new home, Governor Blount moved with his family to Knoxville, the new capital. At first he lived in a plain log-house, but later built a large frame house on the slope between the fort and the river. The new mansion was surrounded by a large yard which Lady Blount kept well adorned with rare flowers. The Governor was ever ready to entertain strangers as well as friends, giving a cordial welcome to the rich and poor alike.

In 1792 Governor Blount met the Indians in council at Coyatee. When he and his escort arrived they saw the American flag waving in the air and two thousand Indians drawn up in two columns ready to receive them. The Indians fired several salutes. They were rejoiced because the Governor had come to distribute their goods and pay their annuity. The Governor, after the distribution of the goods, took advantage of the occasion to remind the chiefs of their frequent violations of their treaty. John Watts, Hanging Maw, and the Breath of Nickajack assured the Governor that their people were for peace. Under a strong guard, Blount then went to Nashville and made a treaty with the Chickasaws and Choctaws, distributing among them their goods and receiving assurance of renewed friendship.

But the Indians, unchecked by their chiefs, were upon the warpath day and night. They soon learned the tactics the officers were ordered to follow and became very bold in their attacks. They fell upon the settlers with shocking barbarity, then hurried beyond the frontiers without fear of being pursued and punished for their crimes. No man understood the Indian's character better than Nolichucky Jack, who was thoroughly convinced that the final peace with the dusky fellows must be achieved by fire and sword, and that it would take battle after battle and expedition after expedition to subdue their passion for warring against the citizens of the Territory. After the Indians had stormed and destroyed Fort Gillespie, it was impossible to repress the citizens of the Territory any longer. Rumors were in air that a large force of Indians intended to strike a heavy blow at the people all along the frontier, and that they were already on the warpath. It was thought that they intended to fall upon Knoxville especially and to seize the arms and ammunition which they knew to be stored there.

Captain Harrison's light-horse had scouted through the country in every direction, but had seen no sign of the Indians. But that very day the chiefs, John Watts and Double Head, led a band of a thousand warriors across the Tennessee below the mouth of the Holston and marched all night in the direction of Knoxville. Seven hundred Creeks were in the band, and one hundred of their number were mounted on fleet horses. They intended to reach Knoxville by daylight, but were delayed in crossing the river and by the bitter rivalry between the two chiefs, Double Head and Van, each of whom aspired to be the leader of the invasion. The chiefs were unable to decide whether they should massacre all the inhabitants in Knoxville, or the men only. Van desired to spare the women and children, but Double Head wished to put all alike to the tomahawk and scalping-knife. In their haste to reach Knoxville, the Indians passed Campbell's Station (in which were twenty families) undisturbed. Onward they rushed, but as they rode out of a valley to the top of a hill, just at sunrise, they heard the roar of a cannon. It was the sunrise gun of the United States troops stationed at Knoxville. This caused the Indians to believe their attack was expected and threw them into confusion and caused them to give up their plan. Near them and in sight was Cavet's Station in which were only three armed men and Mr. Cavet's family. Mortified over the failure of their plans, the Indians attacked this station. The armed men returned the fire and held the warriors at bay for a while. A half-breed Creek who spoke English was sent to Cavet's Station to tell the men that if they would surrender they would be spared and exchanged for Indian prisoners. They yielded, but had scarcely left their door when Double Head and his party fell upon them and murdered them all, save one whose life was spared by Watts. Cavet was afterwards found dead in his garden with seven bullets in his mouth. He had put the bullets there so that he could reload his rifle quickly.

News of the disaster at Cavet's Station was not long in finding its way to Knoxville. Here the fighting force was only forty armed men. They believed the Indians were then marching to attack their fort and resolved to defend themselves or die in the attempt. Leaving two of the oldest men to mould bullets and look to the loading of the guns in the fort, the remainder of the men marched out to a ridge a little more than a mile from Knoxville and stationed themselves about twenty yards apart on the side next to town. On the approach of the Indians, each man was to fire with sure aim and then retreat to the fort and make a final desperate stand. But the Indians never came, and the men returned quietly to their stronghold.

Upon receiving news of the disaster at Cavet's Station, General Sevier, at Ish's Station, hurried out reinforcements. In the meantime, not knowing where the Indians would make the next attack, he sent Captain Harrison across the Holston with his light-horse to discover their movements. The Captain went to the smoldering heap at Cavet's Station and, following the trail of the warriors for some distance, soon found that they had gone south.

In the absence of Blount, Daniel Smith, acting governor of the Territory, gave Governor Sevier permission to follow his favorite mode of fighting the Indians, and Sevier was himself again. Receiving reinforcements he advanced immediately upon the Indians. Crossing the Little Tennessee, he destroyed Estimaula, one of their largest villages, and that night he camped on the banks of the Estimaula River, the horses being hidden in the woods near the camp. His army was very close to the fleeing warriors and he expected them to attempt a night attack. The woods echoed with noises which convinced the General that danger was near. The sentinels were doubled and the troops slept on their arms. Late in the night the warriors came stealthily creeping through the high sedge-grass so near that the sentinels heard them cock their guns. The soldiers fired, the warriors returned the fire, then retired. Next night the camp-fires were left blazing, but the troops camped some distance away. Again the Indians came and fired, but this time into the deserted camping-ground. Seeing their mistake, they again took flight. Next morning General Sevier dashed onward like a hurricane through the choicest part of the Indian country. He even pushed on to the Creek country, leaving only flames and smoke behind. At Etowah, on October 17th, he found the combined forces of the Creeks and Cherokees drawn up ready to dispute the passage of the High Tower River. The

General himself tells the story of the battle that followed in these words:

"On the 17th inst., in the afternoon, we arrived at the forks of Coosa and High Tower rivers. Colonel Kelley was ordered, with a part of his Knox regiment, to endeavor to cross the High Tower. The Creeks and a number of Cherokees had entrenched themselves to obstruct the passage. Colonel Kelly and his party passed down the river, half a mile below the ford, and began to cross at a private place, where there was no ford. Himself and a few others swam over the river. The Indians, discovering this movement, immediately left their entrenchments, and ran down the river to oppose their passage, expecting, as I suppose, the whole intended crossing at the lower place. Captain Evans immediately, with a company of mounted infantry, strained their horses back to the upper ford and began to cross the river. Very few had got to the south bank before the Indians, who had discovered their mistake, returned and received them furiously at the rising of the bank. An engagement instantly took place, and became very warm, and, notwithstanding the enemy were at least four to one in numbers, besides [having] the advantage of the situation, Captain Evans, with his heroic company, put them entirely to flight. They left several dead on the ground, and were seen to carry others off both on foot and horse.... Trails of blood from the wounded were to be seen in every quarter. Their encampment fell into our hands, with a number of their guns, many of which were of the Spanish sort.... The party flogged at High Tower were those which had been out with Watts.... We took and destroyed near three hundred beeves, many of which were of the best and largest kind. Of course, their losing so much provisions must distress them very much. Many women and children might have been taken; but, from motives of humanity, I did not encourage it to be done, and several taken were suffered to make their escape. Your excellency knows the disposition of many who were out on this expedition, and can readily account for this conduct."[1]

Thus ended the last military service of General Sevier. For

nearly twenty years he had been constantly engaged in expensive expeditions against the enemy, yet he never received pay from the government for any of them, except this Etowah campaign. In this last campaign he was serving as an officer of the United States, hence the reason for his receiving pay for himself and his soldiers this time. In thirty-five battles he had wielded his sword and swept the enemy from the battlefield, and so careful was he in all his plans of assault that he lost in all his engagements only fifty-six men. Every time he charged, the ranks of the enemy were broken and victory was his. By his vigilance and swift campaigns with fire and sword, he broke the power of the Creeks and Cherokees and forced them to bury their tomahawks, which they never again dug up to wield against his people.

About this time the Indians of the lower towns along the Tennessee were giving great distress to the settlers along the Cumberland at Nashville. Sevier, now no longer acting upon the defensive, the crippled warriors turned their forces against Robertson, who was still careful to use the defensive tactics. He feared that one battle with the Indians or the death of a Spanish trader might destroy the friendly relations with Spain and put an end to the negotiations for the free navigation of the Mississippi River. One campaign against the towns would break the power of these Indians, and the people clamored to storm them and teach them the lesson that Sevier had taught them at Etowah, but Robertson would not yet consent. Scarcely a week passed for nearly four years without the murder of some settler. The three sons of Valentine Sevier were killed, and Robertson himself was wounded.

Every day the feeling of indignation among the people grew stronger, and Robertson finally decided to follow the example set by Sevier at Etowah. Soon an opportunity came. The Creeks had been stirred up by one of their chiefs, who had falsely reported Robertson as having said, "There has been a great deal of blood spilt in our settlement, and I will come and sweep it clean with your blood." This report

[1] Ramsey's "Annals of Tennessee," p. 587.

caused a general uprising of the Creeks. A force of six hundred Indians invaded the Cumberland Settlement and attacked Buchanan's Station, which was defended by only fifteen men, but by their almost superhuman efforts the Indians were repulsed with heavy loss. A succession of fights followed and the white men determined to give the Lower Towns their Etowah. The Nick-a-jack expedition resulted.

While raising troops for the expedition, the question came, "Who is to be our guide?" and Joseph Brown was selected as the most suitable man. This man's life was an interesting one. When he was only a boy, his father, Colonel James Brown, an officer in the American Revolution, undertook a voyage down the Tennessee to settle upon the Cumberland. He took with him his family, several negroes, and five young men. His boat, built on the Holston, was walled around above the gunwales with oak planks two inches thick. Port holes were made in the sides, and a swivel was placed in the stern for a defense. As soon as they had passed the Chickamauga towns, Indian runners were sent across the mountains to warn the warriors at Nick-a-jack and Running Water of the coming of the boat. The Indians paddled up the river in their canoes to meet the boat. They held up white flags, but this was a ruse, for their guns and tomahawks were concealed in the bottom of their canoes. Brown wheeled his boat and faced them with the swivel, ordering them not to come near. But Van, one of their number, came on board to talk with him, stating that his men only wanted to see where he was going and to trade with him. Accordingly Brown ordered his men not to fire. The Indians then moved up to the boat and began to rob it. Brown asked Van to prevent the mischief, but Van only stated that the headman was then away and that as soon as he returned the goods would all be restored. Then a dirty, black-looking savage with a sword in his hand took young Joseph by the arm and was about to kill him, when Mr. Brown interfered. Joseph was released, and Mr. Brown turned to see what else was being done. As soon as Brown's back was turned, the brutal savage drew his sword and cut his head nearly half off, and another Indian threw him overboard. Poor little Joseph saw his unfortunate father thrown overboard and ran to tell his brothers. The scene that followed was horrible. Little Joseph, his poor mother, and the rest of the family left alive, were taken prisoners and scattered among the Creek and Cherokee towns as slaves.

Little Joseph expected to be murdered. The Indians really intended to kill him and had stripped off his clothes when an old French woman begged them not to kill him there nor along the road she had to pass in carrying her water from the spring. While they were muttering and stripping him of his clothes, the poor lad fell upon his knees and cried, like the dying Saint Stephen, "Lord Jesus, into thy hands I commend my spirit." He was spared, but had a hard life among the Indians. Holes were bored in his ears, and his hair was cut short, leaving only a scalp-lock. He was compelled to wear Indian clothing which exposed his body to the burning sun; and he was sent to hoe corn in the hot sun till he was blistered with the heat. He at first became sick and faint and would have perished had it not been for the approach of a rain cloud which drove the laborers from the field. After several years of slavery and untold hardships, the lad and his mother and sisters were rescued by General Sevier.

But Joseph had learned well the locations of the lower towns, and after a lapse of a few years he was employed as a guide of an army which was determined to crush the power of the warriors who had killed his father and enslaved his mother.

Brown found a route from Nashville to the Indian towns, and Major Ore began the march. Crossing Duck River below the Old Stone Fort, an Indian monument of some archaeological interest, below Manchester, Tennessee, the army pushed across the Cumberland Mountain and reached the Tennessee, near the mouth of the Sequatchie. Here the soldiers constructed rafts and canoes and crossed the Tennessee in the rear of the town. The troops were formed into two divisions, one to go above Nick-a-jack, the other below, to make a simultaneous attack. The Indians felt so secure that they had no sentinels posted. There was only one way for them to escape to the river and this was by a small creek that emptied into it below the town. All this Brown carefully explained to the soldiers.

At the first fire of the soldiers, the Indians took alarm and made a sudden rush for the river. As they huddled together, the soldiers poured streams of lead into their crowded ranks and but few escaped. Running Water next fell, and the power of the Indians was completely broken. Thus ended the last struggle between the Indians and the white settlers for the possession of this fertile region.

A quiet, peaceable, liberty-loving, industrious, God-fearing people now bore the banners of civilization through the western wilderness and converted the forests into waving fields of golden grain. Their example was slowly followed by the Indians. They abandoned to a great extent the arts of war and began to till the soil.

From this time till 1796, the population increased with wonderful rapidity. Scarcely a day passed without the arrival of families of immigrants. The towns grew as if by magic. In the older settlements more stately mansions were built, and the manner of living became more refined. Post offices were established and mail was regularly received from the seaboard, but it took a long time to get a reply to a letter addressed to any one living east of the Alleghanies, as the carrier was many days in making his trip. Besides, the postage rates were so high that very few letters were written. When a letter was received at the post office, it often passed through many hands before it reached its owner.

On November 5th, 1791, a newspaper was published by Mr. George Roulston, first at Rogersville, and soon afterwards moved to Knoxville, where it took the name of "The Knoxville Gazette." It was the first newspaper west of the Alleghanies.

Everywhere the people manifested a fresh religious zeal and enthusiasm, and the churches vied with each other in spreading the doctrines of their faiths. The Methodists began to hold their conferences in the troublous times of the State of Franklin and their "circuit riders" did much for the spiritual welfare of the pioneers and much to make them better citizens. The Baptists and the Presbyterians were equally zealous in their services. The people were careful in their attendance at church, often going a distance of fifteen miles to attend services.

In the older settlements, the schools were growing better, and more interest was being shown in education. The example and efforts of Doctor Doak were an inspiration to the citizens. General Sevier took an active part in establishing Washington College and Blount College, the latter of which has grown into the University of Tennessee, one of the best in the South. There was set in motion at this time that interest in education which is today the life of Tennessee.

The sports and pastimes of the people were about the same as in earlier days. Log-rollings, quilting-bees, corn-huskings, shooting matches, hunting-trips, and horse-racing were time-honored sports which brought the people together on many an occasion. A wedding was an event of importance. The ceremony, very simple in kind, was performed sometimes at church, but more often at the bride's home. Sometimes a bountiful supper was served, followed by a social gathering of relatives and friends. There were no buggies and carriages to accommodate the happy pair; when they took a wedding trip, it was on horseback. It frequently happened that the young husband had only a single horse, and in such case he would take his young wife up behind him.

This was nearly a century before the telephone, yet it is astonishing to observe how rapidly news traveled through the country. Every family was careful to entertain strangers. The larger and wealthier families living near the road would often send a courteous old slave to invite traveling strangers to stay all night and tell them the news. Many a night they would sit up till late hours telling thrilling tales, perchance of some ancestor's voyage, beset with storms and shipwrecks, or of the swift campaigns of Nolichucky Jack against the Indians.

Such was the life among the people of the Territory. The men were honest and lived by the sweat of the brow. Their labor in the out-door air gave them strong, healthful bodies, and it was not an uncommon thing for a man to live to the ripe old age of one hundred years. From this sturdy, honest people many prominent Americans have sprung, men whose names adorn the pages of our nation's history.

Everywhere the hardy settlers were blessed with peace and plenty. It was an Arcadia with its barns filled with plenty, the schools flourishing, religion prevailing, and the people happy. There was marrying and giving in marriage, and the growth of the population was so rapid that the census of 1795 showed that there were more than sixty thousand white people in the Territory—more than the required number to entitle the Territory to become a State.

Chapter XIII

The Closing Days

The proposition of creating a new State out of the Territory was left by Congress to a vote of the people. The era of good feeling that had existed under the Territory caused many people to oppose the formation of a new State, but the wiser everywhere were enthusiastic for the change. The reason was obvious. They loved Governor Blount, but they did not like to live under even good laws and the best of rulers in the selection of which they had no voice. As it was, they had no voice in making the laws and no vote in the Presidential elections.

On January 11th, 1796, a convention met at Knoxville to form a constitution. There were by this time eleven counties in the Territory, and each of these counties furnished five men to the convention. On the first day of the meeting, Governor William Blount was chosen president of the convention, and the other officers were elected. The next day the actual work of the convention began with a prayer and a sermon delivered by Reverend Samuel Carrick. Perfect harmony prevailed among the members. It was proposed by Andrew Jackson that the new State be named after the magnificent river which winds across the Territory. This river was first called the Cherokee, but gradually become known as the Tenasee, or Tennessee. From the convention, a committee of two members from each county was selected to draw up a bill of rights and a constitution for the State. So well did this committee do its work that Mr. Jefferson declared it to be "the least imperfect and most republican" constitution among the States. The whole session lasted only twenty-seven days, and it was marked throughout by rigid economy on the part of the members. They were paid $1.50 a day for their services and 3½ cents a mile for traveling expenses; they paid the clerks $2.50 a day, and the door-keeper $2.00 a day, and the entire incidental expenses amounted to only $12.62.

After the work of the convention was finished, Governor Blount issued an order for the election of Governor and members of the Legislature for the new State. The people responded to the order, and the first Legislature of Tennessee met at Knoxville, the first capital of Tennessee, March 28th, 1796. The election returns, examined by the Legislature, showed that John Sevier was elected Governor without opposition.

On March 30th, 1796, Mr. Sevier was sworn into office in the presence of both houses of the Legislature, by Judge Joseph Anderson. The Legislature then elected William Maclin, Secretary of State; Landon Carter, Treasurer of Washington and Hamilton Districts; William Black, Treasurer of Miro District; John McNairy, William Blount, and Archibald Roane, Judges of the Supreme Court; Hopkins Lacy, John Lowry, and Howell Tatum, Attorneys for the State; William Blount and William Cooke, Senators in Congress.

In Congress there was much opposition to the admission of the Territory. It was claimed by some that the people of the Territory could not take the census themselves, but that it must be done by an act of Congress. It was suspected that the friends of Mr. Jefferson desired the admission of Tennessee that its vote might be cast for him to succeed Mr. Adams as President. But the bill finally passed the Senate. On June 1st, 1796, President Washington signed the act of Congress that created the State of Tennessee, which, on account of the vast number of volunteers in war, has been very appropriately called the Volunteer State. The Senators were reelected in August, and Andrew Jackson was elected the first Representative in Congress from Tennessee. Jackson was a man of iron and an ardent supporter of Mr. Jefferson's party. In fact the majority of the people in the State were of this party.

The first message sent by Governor Sevier to the Legislature was brief:

"Gentlemen of the Senate and House of Representatives: The high and honorable appointment conferred upon me by the free suffrage of my countrymen fills my breast with gratitude, which, I trust, my future life will manifest. I take this early opportunity to express, through you, my thanks in the strongest terms of acknowledgment. I shall labor to discharge with fidelity the trust reposed in me; and, if such my exertions should prove satisfactory, the first wish of my heart will be gratified.

"Gentlemen, accept of my best wishes for your individual and public happiness; and, relying upon your wisdom and patriotism, I have no doubt but the result of your deliberations will give permanency and success to our new system of government, so wisely calculated to secure the liberty and advance the happiness and prosperity of our fellow citizens."

By a wise stroke of policy, Governor Sevier began to reconcile his enemies by bestowing favors upon them. Among the first officers appointed was John Tipton, his bitterest enemy. The new Governor ordered a seal for the State. In this seal, the cotton-plant, the sheaf of wheat, the plow and the sailing vessel were adopted as emblems of the great resources of Tennessee. He secured compensation from the United States government for the soldiers who had fought in the Etowah campaign.

The white men were encroaching daily upon the Indians' lands, and the relations between the Indians and the white men were again becoming sorely strained. The treaty between the United States and Spain, in the previous year, had secured the free navigation of the Mississippi River and put an end to Spanish intrigues; and the Governor, by the help of Congress, settled the difficulty without bloodshed.

After his election to the Senate, William Blount was accused of having entered into a conspiracy with the British to draw Tennessee out of the Union and help England organize an empire in the great Southwest. On this charge he was expelled from the Senate, July 8th, 1797. An officer of the United States was sent to Knoxville to arrest him and take him to Philadelphia for trial. Blount refused to go; the officer himself could not take him, and the men summoned to help arrest him absolutely refused to do so. So the matter ended. An investigation proved to the Senate that no case could be sustained against Mr. Blount. He was at once elected to the State Senate and was made Speaker of that body. He died at Knoxville, March 21st, 1800, and was buried in the yard of the First Presbyterian Church in that city.

In 1798 Sevier was re-elected Governor without opposition. These years of the Governor were busy and full of care for the welfare of the new commonwealth. He encouraged manufacturing and commerce, for he knew that the wealth of a country depends upon its skillful laborers and its trade relations. There were no railroads, of course, to carry on trade with other States, but boats went down the Tennessee and the Mississippi to New Orleans with heavy cargoes, and wagon trains went regularly to the eastern cities with loads of farm products and bought goods and articles of every kind to supply the wants of the people. Schools were growing better everywhere, books were more plentiful, and the people read more than they had formerly done.

In the midst of peace and prosperity, Sevier's second term of office expired in 1799; and the people elected him again. His third term was characterized by the same degree of prosperity. Three times in succession had he been elected Governor without opposition, and now, according to the constitution, he was ineligible till some other man had served a term. So, in the election that followed, Archibald Roane was elected.

Governor Sevier now retired to his farm south of Knoxville, where he remained for two years in the enjoyments of his home. He lived the life of a plain country gentleman. He went to church regularly. His farm was tilled by his slaves, and it was his chief vocation to superintend their work. As he rode among them, his slaves greeted him courteously, for they had a deep affection for him. Scarcely a day passed at his hospitable home without the entertainment of some friend. Sometimes it was an Indian chief or a dusky warrior against whom he had drawn his sword in a more evil time; but the Indians ever remembered Nolichucky Jack as a *good man*. But it was more generally the battle-scarred veterans who had come to visit their old general, whom they had never forgotten to love. Many a night did they sit before the roaring fire in the huge fireplace, recounting the exploits of Sevier's thirty-five battles and thirty-five victories.

At the expiration of Roane's term of office, the people again called for the re-election of Sevier. Again the "Good Old Governor" was elected and again he assumed the weight of responsibility as the chief magistrate of the State.

Although Sevier was elected by the popular vote, there were those who, jealous of his popularity, tried to destroy his political favor by circulating false reports about him. They accused him of speculation in land-warrants and even of forgery. John Tipton, a member of the Legislature at the time, made strenuous exertions for his downfall. These reports caused a committee of investigation to be appointed to look into the matter. This committee found the charges to be without foundation. Sevier's popularity seems not to have been affected by these efforts to injure his reputation. But his indignation was aroused against Andrew Jackson, whom he had appointed Judge of the Superior Court. Jackson was of a very different temper from Sevier. Sevier's temper was fiery, but he was ever ready and eager to atone for any wrong he had done, while, on the other hand, Jackson rarely forgave an enemy.

Jackson was so bold in his attacks upon Sevier's character that the old Governor became deeply angered and used some abusive language in his speeches about Jackson. Not long after the State election, Sevier and Jackson met on the public square in Knoxville, where Jackson was holding court. A quarrel ensued and Sevier accused Jackson of having been the prime-mover of the attacks upon his reputation, and further made a reference to an incident in Jackson's domestic life, upon which point Jackson was very sensitive. Jackson tried to attack Sevier on the spot, but was restrained through the intervention of his friends. The next day Jackson challenged Sevier to fight a duel.

Dueling was a somewhat common practice of those early days. When a challenge was received, it was considered unmanly and even cowardly to refuse to accept it. Each of the incensed men selected some favorite friend for his second, and the time and place for the duel were arranged by these seconds. Everything being in readiness, the duelists, accompanied by their respective seconds, met upon the selected ground. Men were sure marksmen in those days. Previous to the day set for the duel, the antagonists often spent much time at practicing with their pistols. When the hour came, each man took his place at a specified distance apart from the other. Here they stood, their pistols pointing towards the ground. There was silence for a moment; then the silence was broken by the order, "Fire!" Such was the duel as understood by both Sevier and Jackson. But Sevier wrote in a firm hand the following reply to Jackson's challenge:

"Knoxville, Oct. 2, 1803.
"Sir, yours to-day, by Andrew Whithe, Esq., I have received, and am pleased with the contents, so far as respects a personal interview.

"Your ungentlemanly and gasconading conduct of yesterday, and, indeed, at all other times heretofore, have unmasked you to me and to the world. The voice of the Assembly has made you a Judge, and this alone renders you worthy of my notice, or that of any other gentleman. To the office I have respect, and this only makes you worthy of notice.

"I shall wait on you with pleasure at any time and place not within the State of Tennessee, attended by my friend, with pistols, presuming you know nothing about the use of any other arms. Georgia, Virginia and North Carolina are in our vicinity, and we can easily repair to either of those places and conveniently retire into the inoffending government. You cannot mistake me or my meaning.

"Hon. A. Jackson."

"Yours, etc., etc.,
"JOHN SEVIER.

Jackson insisted upon fighting the duel near Knoxville, and, of course, was not pleased with Sevier's reply. But Sevier would not consent to violate the laws of his State and again wrote Jackson: "An interview within the State you know I have denied. Anywhere outside, you have nothing to do but to name the place and I will the time. I have some regard for the laws of the State over which I have the honor to preside, although you, a Judge, appear to have none."

It seemed that a duel was inevitable; but, through negotiations of friends on both sides, matters were finally adjusted, and the two heroes were induced to join hands in friendship.

During his first succession of terms of office, Governor Sevier undertook to build in Knoxville a brick mansion for his residence. After the walls had been raised above the basement, he gave up the plan and sold his property; it was too expensive for his income. The building was finished by the purchaser and is standing to-day in sight of St. John's Episcopal Church, Knoxville.

Sevier continued to live on his plantation, and his friends, rich and poor, continued to share his bountiful hospitality. Distinguished visitors to this country from abroad were sometimes hospitably entertained at his simple country home. On one occasion, three sons of the Duke of Orleans, Louis Philippe and two brothers, were entertained by Governor and Mrs. Sevier. In fact, it took about all his salary, in addition to the resources of his plantation, to enable him to keep up his unlimited hospitality and expensive entertainments of all who chose to lodge with him. Is it a wonder, then, that he was always poor?[1]

Governor Sevier, with his family, attended church at Lebanon, about four miles east of Knoxville. Reverend Samuel Carrick was the pastor. On such occasions Sevier laid aside his military uniform, wearing his three-cornered hat and citizen's clothes. At church he had his usual cordial greetings for his friends and always listened to the sermon with a grave, reverential demeanor, for he held the most sacred regard for everything moral and religious. But he never became a member of any church, as he did not approve of the doctrinal opinions which he had thus far been taught. In his old age, when flattered by friends on his useful career and great achievements for western civilization, he informed them that he was only an instrument in the hands of Providence and was always led and guided by His Infinite Goodness.

In 1805 and again in 1807 he was reelected, and so six more years of his life were spent in the gubernatorial office. Again he became ineligible and sought the retirement of the quiet country life. But his friends, feeling grateful for the great services he had rendered to the State and to America in his earlier years, wished to bestow other honors upon him. So, in 1811, they elected him to Congress, and again in 1813, and 1815.

While he was in Congress, the War of 1812 was declared and waged. During this time he was usually a silent worker, but accomplished much. From his long experience in the tactics of war, he was placed on the Committee of Military Affairs and rendered valuable services to the nation during the whole war. President Madison offered him a generalship in the army, but Sevier declined to accept it.

In 1815, the year of the battle of New Orleans, President Madison appointed Sevier a commissioner to run the boundary line of the lands which the Creeks had just ceded to the United States. In June, he left his Bonny Kate, never again to see her. He was in his seventy-first year, and his body was

[1] The following, given to Doctor Draper in 1844 by George Washington Sevier, son of John Sevier shows another cause of the General's straighed circumstances: "Notwithstanding he had settled in Tennessee at an early day and had much of the fine lands in the country, yet he died comparatively poor. From his natural, obliging way, he had become security for friends and had many thousand dollars to pay of security debts, and in order to meet them sold several thousand acres of his choicest lands for 40 cents an acre that have since commanded well-nigh as many dollars."—Draper MSS.

weakened by his lifetime of struggles and hardships. While at work in the Creek country, he contracted a fever.

During the time of his illness he lay in his tent near Fort Decatur, Alabama, and Bonny Kate knew nothing of his confinement and suffering. For fifteen days he suffered with the fortitude of a Christian hero; then, on September 24, 1815, surrounded by anxious, watchful friends, he drew his last breath.

He was buried with the honors of war, by the troops commanded by Captain William Walker, on the east bank of the Tallapoosa River, at an Indian village called Tuckabatchee, near Fort Decatur, Alabama. His grave was subsequently marked by a simple grave-stone on which was carved, "John Sevier."

Unaware of Sevier's illness at Fort Decatur, the Tennesseans had a few weeks before re-elected him to Congress without opposition. At the news of his death the whole State mourned. The Legislature of Tennessee passed a resolution that each of the State officials wear for thirty days a badge of mourning out of respect for his memory.

Strange to say, the citizens of Tennessee neglected the grave of John Sevier for many years. Not until 1889 was the body of the first governor of the State brought back to Tennessee. In June of that year the body was interred in the court-house yard at Knoxville with imposing ceremonies. Today a beautiful marble monument towers above his grave, bearing the following inscriptions: "John Sevier, Nolichucky Jack, September 23rd, 1744; September 24th, 1815; pioneer, soldier, statesman, and one of the founders of the republic; Governor of the State of Franklin; six terms Governor of Tennessee; four times elected to Congress; the typical pioneer who conquered the wilderness and fashioned the State; a projector and hero of King's Mountain; thirty-five battles, thirty-five victories; his Indian war-cry, 'Here they are! come on, boys, come on!'"

Mankind delights to honor with monuments, busts, statues, and paintings, the heroes whom the world has learned to love; but the most intrinsic mementos to the world are the noble deeds of the heroes themselves. But let the world sing its paeans of praises; for they are grand and glorious to hear. The painter, the poet, and the sculptor have built beautiful memorials to these great and good heroes. May the day come when they shall adorn the Hall of Fame with a fitting memorial to that good man, that true hero, that unselfish statesman, "Nolichucky Jack"!